MAO'S
LONG MARCH

I. G. Edmonds

MAO'S LONG MARCH

AN EPIC OF
HUMAN COURAGE

MACRAE SMITH COMPANY
Philadelphia

Copyright © 1973 by I. G. Edmonds
Library of Congress Catalog Card Number 72-12337
Manufactured in the United States of America

Published simultaneously in Canada by
George J. McLeod, Limited, Toronto

7304

Library of Congress Cataloging in Publication Data

Edmonds, I. G.
  Mao's Long March.

  SUMMARY: Describes the events of the 6,000-mile march un-
dertaken by Mao Tse-tung and his Communist followers as they
retreated before the forces of Chiang Kai-shek.
  Bibliography: p.
  1. Long March, 1934-1935—Juvenile literature. [1. Long
March, 1934-1935. 2. China—History]
I. Title.
DS777.47.E35   951.04′2   72-12337
ISBN 0-8255-3004-0

Dedication

To Annette and Reilco

Contents

THE ROUTES OF THE RED ARMY

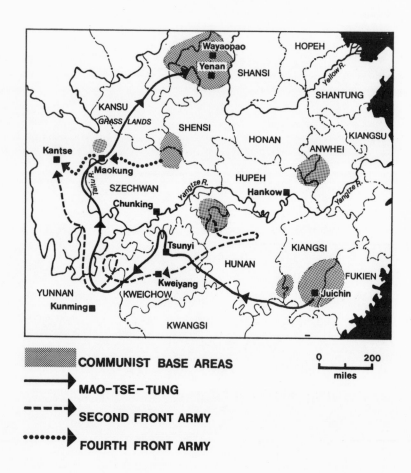

COMMUNIST BASE AREAS

MAO-TSE-TUNG

SECOND FRONT ARMY

FOURTH FRONT ARMY

Introduction

Authors who write about Communism and its people, either pro or con, for the most part write in terms of right and wrong. Communism and Communists, one would conclude, are either all bad or all good. There seems to be no in-between —no shades between absolute wickedness and absolute goodness. Yet, as one side belabors the other, both seem to agree, in part, at least, about what the Chinese call the *Chang Cheng* and Westerners translate as the Long March. Although people may disagree on the motives and results of the Long March, all speak of it with awe as one of history's great examples of human courage and endurance. The facts about it are awe-inspiring.

In brief the Long March was simply this: In October 1934 the Chinese Communist Party was facing total extermination by the armies of Chiang Kai-shek. One hundred thousand Communists broke through the trap and marched to safety in a barren area of China six thousand miles from where they started. This distance is reckoned along a straight line of march. However, maneuvering and backtracking probably made the march closer to eight thousand miles. This meant that the marchers had to average nearly twenty-two miles a day while fighting a constant, running battle against an enemy who had sworn to exterminate them. Extermination, in this case, is not a literary word chosen for its suspenseful effect. It was a word chosen by Chiang Kai-shek, who called his attack the "Fifth Red Bandit Extermination Campaign."

When they were not fighting the enemy, the marchers fought nature. They climbed and fought at altitudes where the air was so rare that even slight exertion left them gasping for breath. They were blown off mountains to their deaths by cyclonic winds. They were engulfed by quicksand marshes hidden under a unique sea of grass. They struggled through torrential rains in the subtropic plains and then climbed mountains where it was so cold that weary men stooped to rest and froze in their squatted position. But still they went on.

In trying to explain the truly superhuman efforts of those who made the Long March, Communist and anti-Communist writers alike reach back into history to find parallels. They compare it to the *Anabasis*—the desperate fighting retreat of the ten thousand Greeks under Xenophon who had to march from present-day Iraq to Turkey to escape the Persian army, and to Hannibal's march across the Alps to attack Rome, and to Bolivar's heroic march up the Orinoco River and over the Andes into Venezuela. As a matter of comparison, Xenophon marched 1,500 miles, Hannibal's grueling climb over the Alps was less than a thousand miles, and Bolivar's struggle through jungle swamps and icy mountain trails covered about two thousand miles. The Chinese who made the Long March faced the same natural dangers and faced them for at least four times the distance.

Here is what various writers, pro-Communist and anti-Communist, have said about the Long March.

"The Long March, or marches, were epic feats of arms." This is from the American Heritage Press's *Communism Takes China.*

"The 6,000-mile Long March was an epic of human perserverence." The Editors of *Life* Magazine, in *China,* a volume of the Life World Library.

The Long March was a savage ordeal that stands out in Chinese Communist history as an emotional mountain peak." Theodore H. White in *"Thunder Out China.*

"However one may feel about the Reds and what they represent politically. . .it is impossible to deny recognition to their Long March—the *Chang Cheng,* as they call it—as one of the great exploits of military history." Edgar Snow, in *Red Star Over China.*

"Their accomplishment of making a six-thousand mile retreat and arriving with morale as high as or higher then when they had started almost makes Hannibal's crossing of the Alps and Napoleon's Russian campaigns seem like summer picnics." Robert Goldston, in *The Rise of Red China.*

"Neither facts nor figures, nor the names of a hundred rivers and mountains, can ever explain the historical significance of the Long March of the Red Army. Nor can they describe the tenacity and determination nor the suffering of the hundred thousand men who took part in it." Agnes Smedley, a Communist sympathizer who wrote *China's Red Army Marches.*

"The Long March was one of the great military feats of history. It also was an impressive example of the tenacity of faith." John Roderick, Far East Bureau Chief for the Associated Press.

The Long March was similar in spirit, although not in actions, to the Japanese tale of the Forty-Seven Ronin. In the Ronin story a group of men gave up family, home, friends and honor, willingly embracing utter debasement in order to revenge their master. Their objective was not revenge for revenge's sake but fulfillment of honor. During Japan's militaristic Bushido period, Westerners were told they could not understand the Japanese character unless they understood the spirit that motivated the Forty-Seven Ronin.

Likewise, one cannot understood the spirit that brought Communism out of abject defeat to rule the largest (in population) nation on earth unless one can understand what it was that kept hungry, ragged men stumbling ahead along the icy trails of the Great Snow Mountains, swinging hand-over-hand across the Tatu Gorge, and struggling through rain and marshes while enemy planes bombed from overhead and enemy guns blazed at every turn of the road.

While many famous Chinese participated in the Long March and made outstanding contributions—men like Chu Teh, Lin Piao and Chou En-lai—in the end it proved to be Mao Tse-tung's march. His efforts during that time were paramount in revitalizing the Chinese Communist Party. China would not be Communist today if there had been no Long March. The political events that are interwoven with the heroic adventures related here should support this statement.

My account of the Long March is intended not to be either pro-Communist or anti-Communist but to be as objective a telling as possible of what happened. All the major points and events recorded here can be documented.

1

Flight from Kiangsi

Everyone knew something important was going to happen. Spies for Chiang Kai-shek's Nationalist Army carried back word of feverish preparations going on inside the Communist soviet that controlled two-thirds of Kiangsi province in that part of China known as the lower Yangtze region. It lay directly north of Canton.

The reports claimed that huge stores of rice and barley were being sacked so that they could be quickly thrown across the backs of pack animals. Horses were being assembled at remount stations. Seamstresses were working until they dropped with fatigue to make "sausage bags," which were long sacks in which individual soldiers carried two-weeks' rations on their backs. Communist officials were moving hastily from one secret meeting to another.

There was uneasiness among the people of Juichin, the soviet capital, as the preparations to leave continued, but there was no panic. Kiangsi had been the seat of war since 1929, and it was now 1934. However, the Communist position had never been so desperate as it was now. Four times before, Chiang had launched what he called "Red Bandit Extermination Campaigns." Each time the Communists had managed to outmaneuver Chiang's troops. This new campaign was different. Chiang was relying on the able advice of General Von Seeckt, former chief-of-staff of the German Army. Von Seeckt's plan abandoned direct thrusts into Communist territory. Instead, the soviets (which were small Communist states) were surrounded.

Chiang's army was building a series of blockhouses around the Kiangsi soviet, which was the largest of the independent states under Communist control. Thousands of smaller fortifications were constructed between these major military points to prevent the enemy from infiltrating into the Nationalist lines. The fortifications were backed by newly built roads to provide an ability to maneuver rapidly. The result was a blockade that slowly strangled the Kiangsi soviet.

The end came slowly to Kiangsi for two reasons. One was that Chiang did not press an attack. He gradually squeezed in his circle of steel about the soviet. The other reason was that Kiangsi is in a subtropical zone and is rich agriculturally. Two rice crops are grown there each year. Tangerines are abundant, and the raising of livestock is a major industry. In addition, the province has both iron and coal, which the Communists used in a large arsenal in Juichin to manufacture arms. All this provided an economic base that reduced the effectiveness of the blockade.

The Communist "republic" in 1934 encompassed two-thirds of Kiangsi and, according to Mao Tse-tung's claim, half of its population. The nine million people had lived under the government of Mao Tse-tung and his military partner, Chu Teh, for five years. Dissidents had been eliminated. Those who remained were staunch Communists. An invader faced not only the Red Army, but also the entire population of the province.

As the Nationalists' iron ring tightened in other areas, the Chinese Communist Party's Central Committee fled to Kiangsi. Mao was president of the Kiangsi soviet but subordinate to the Central Committee. In later years some propagandists would imply that Mao founded the Communist Party in 1921 and ruled its destiny as a beloved leader for ever after. That is not true, and Mao's own early writing gives a clear picture of his opposition to the basic policies of the Central Committee. Why writers try to give a false impression is not clear. What Mao Tse-tung did accomplish for the Chinese Communist Party is sufficient to place him among the Communist immortals for all time to come. He needs no propagandist's gilding.

By the September of 1934 it was clear that the Kiangsi soviet could not hold out much longer. While the food supply was still adequate, the economy was suffering badly because raw materials for the factories could not be brought through the blockade, nor could finished products find a market. Worst of all, the soviet had no salt, and the absence of this basic essential of life had reached the critical point.

There was a meeting of the Central Committee to consider the desperate situation. Mao was not a member of the Committee, which was composed of the "28 Bolsheviks" who had been trained in Russia and the "Whampoa Clique," which was made up of army officers who had originally been trained at the Chinese military academy under their present enemy Chiang Kai-shek.

Although president of the Kiangsi soviet, Mao did not participate in the historic meeting. A decision was reached—Mao not dissenting for once—that the army would have to abandon Kiangsi or be destroyed. Chiang Kai-shek was obviously preparing for a final assault soon. The bombing and strafing from the small but efficient Nationalist air force had increased. The Red Army alone had suffered 60,000 casualties, and the number of civilians killed was twice that.

Once the decision to move was made, the Central Committee acted swiftly. The original plan did not envision the six-thousand-mile epic march that finally developed.

Speaking of this period, Robert Payne, in his biography of Mao Tse-tung, quotes Mao as saying, "If you mean did we have any exact plans, the answer is that we had none. We intended to break out of the encirclement and join up with other soviets."

Nym Wales (in *Red Dust*) quotes Hsu Meng-chiu, historian for the Long March, as saying, "The original plan was to break through the blockade by surprise and go west to Hunan to join with Ho Lung's Second Front Army."

Further proof that remote Yenan in Shensi province was not in the planners' minds is a remark Mao made to Communist writer Agnes Smedley in 1938. Miss Smedley had complimented Mao on the choice of Yenan as a base. The Communist leader replied, "We didn't pick it." The choice in fact, was forced upon them by circumstances that arose in connection with the march. It was not until they were halfway along that Mao, finally in complete charge, set the final goal.

In the meantime, there was the difficult problem of breaking through the ring of steel that Chiang Kai-shek and General Von Seeckt had forged around the Kiangsi soviet. Chu Teh, commander-in-chief under the Military Council, did not underestimate the difficulties. They had just fought a bitter battle at Kwangchang on the Fukien-Kiangsi frontier, which had left 4,000 dead and 20,000 wounded on the Communist side. The terrible attrition of that battle had convinced the last wavering member of the Central Committee that to remain in Kiangsi any longer would be total disaster.

Preparations were speeded up. The arsenal was dismantled. Some of its equipment was packed to take along on the march. The rest was dispersed into the Kiangsi hills and buried. Hospitals were also moved into the mountains to care for as many as possible of the 20,000 men wounded in the Fukien border battle. Guns were provided for the patients so that they could infiltrate into Nationalist-held territory as partisans after they recovered.

The army began to move on October 13. Those who would make the march and those who would remain had already been given orders. The army units fighting on the various fronts had been pulled back and replaced by partisan peasant fighters. The partisans were ordered to hold the line until the bulk of the army had smashed through the Nationalists' defenses. Then they were to hide their weapons and go back to their primary duty as farmers on the land. When another opportunity presented itself, the farmers would turn again into soldiers.

The army units converged on Yutu, a large town south of the soviet capital Juichin. In keeping with their time-honored strategy, the army made every effort to confuse the enemy. They made it appear that their goal was an attack to the east which they hoped would break through the blockade to some salt wells. Chiang Kai-shek was well aware of the salt shortage in Kiangsi.

Different members of the march have given different dates for the start of it, ranging from October 12 through November 4. These variations are probably due to the fact that different units moved at different times to make the rendezvous at Yutu, and each teller was referring to his own personal part of the great adventure.

The best guess is that the command to march was given on the night of October 18. It was cloudy, and Chiang Kai-shek's reconnaissance planes could not scout their movements. As the columns moved out of Yutu, the movement was more like a migration than a retreat. There were about 70,000 actual soldiers. A description of them handed down by an officer who made the march said, "Each man carried five pounds of ration rice and each had a shoulder pole from which hung either two small boxes of ammunition or hand grenades, or big kerosene cans filled with our most essential machinery or tools. Each man's pack contained a blanket or quilt, one quilted winter uniform [in addition to the summer uniform he wore], and three pairs of strong cloth shoes with thick rope soles tipped and heeled with metal.

"The people also gave us presents of dried vegetables, peppers, or such things. Each man had a drinking cup, a pair of chopsticks thrust into his puttees, and a needle and thread caught on the underside of the peak of his cap. All men wore big sun-rain hats made of bamboo with oiled paper between the two thin layers, and many had paper umbrellas stuck in their packs. Each man carried a rifle. Everyone going on the Long March was dressed and equipped the same."

The fact that these troops were loaded down like coolies with supplies showed that they were in the center column. The army marched in three parallel columns in the beginning. In the center column were a student brigade; the headquarters, with members of the Central Committee; the supply corps; the medical corps, whose nurses were mostly preteenage boys; the propaganda department, whose members carried pieces of a printing press and fonts of type on their backs; and tailors who similarly carried their sewing machines on their backs.

The right and left flank guards carried only their weapons, a sausage bag of rations, and back packs, so that they could maneuver rapidly to protect the center column, which, in addition to the heavily laden soldiers, had 30,000 porters carrying food and bales of supplies and ammunition. The rear guard was another lightly equipped corps led at first by Tung

Ching-tan and later by the brilliant Lo Ping-hui, one of the trickiest of all the commanders under General Chu Teh.

Only the highest-ranking officials rode horses. The rest of the animals were used for packing. Chu Teh, as commander-in-chief, had a horse, but he preferred to walk most of the way. Chou En-lai, the president of the Military Council, rode, as did Lin Piao, commander of one of the armies. Mao Tse-tung also preferred to walk in the beginning. Walking close behind him was his wife, Ho Tzu-hun. Their three small children, too young to make the march, were left with peasants. Later, when Mao searched for them, the children had disappeared.

Tiny Ho Tzu-hun was one of twenty-six women in the march. Most of the few allowed to go along were wives of the high officials. The rest were nurses. The only children along were the "Little Devils," war orphans who had grown up with the army. They served as messengers, as orderlies for the officers, and as nurses.

The March began at night. The central column held fast to a straight advance, while the two flank corps maneuvered to confuse the enemy. Spies reported that Chiang Kai-shek suspected the army of heading west to disguise their true intent, which the Nationalist leader thought would be another attack at government positions on the Fukien frontier, where so many men had been killed in early October.

Instead, Chu Teh suddenly pulled in the flanking corps and rammed a spearlike charge straight through the Nationalists' iron ring of blockhouses and machine-gun nests. The attack was sudden and backed by complete surprise, but even so the carnage was frightful. Without stopping, the Red Army smashed into the second line of defense set up by the Whites (as they termed the Chinese soldiers of Chiang Kai-shek).

The second line of defense was less well defended. The Reds broke through it more easily than they did through the line of blockhouses. Then Chu Teh swung them back, while the central column was still pouring through the breach in the Nationalists' line, and attacked the enemy from the rear. The White Army fell back in confusion. The rest of the Red Army went through, heading up through the rough, mountainous country toward Hunan.

For the next five days they marched only at night. Nationalist planes combed the skies during the daylight hours, roaring low to strafe and bomb any target they could see. At the same time the rear guard was fighting an almost constant battle with the pursuing Nationalists. Men were dying by the thousands. The Red Army lost five thousand dead in the first ten days of the march. They claimed to have killed three times that number of Nationalists, but Chiang had plenty of reinforcements to throw into his depleted ranks. The Red Army's only chance to get new members was to break through the massed enemy troops in Hunan province and join with the soviet operated by General Ho Lung in northern Hunan. Their chance of making it appeared more grim with each passing day.

Then, almost miraculously, the heavy fighting ceased. Low clouds and rain grounded the Nationalist air force. The struggling Red Army started climbing into the Nanling Mountains, which ran along the frontiers of Kiangsi, Hunan and Kwangtung provinces. Chu Teh, despite the near exhaustion of his troops, ordered a forced march to put them as far as possible ahead of the enemy before the weather improved.

"We now marched four hours and rested four hours," Hsu Meng-Chiu told Nym Wales, speaking of this period in the Long March. "We did this for three full days and moved 120 miles."

Another soldier, whose name was not given, told Agnes Smedley, "Night marching is wonderful . . . When no enemy troops were near, whole companies would sing, and others would answer. If it was a black night and the enemy was far away, we made torches from pine branches or frayed bamboo.

Then it was truly beautiful. When at the foot of a mountain we could look up and see a long column of lights coiling like a fiery dragon up the mountain side."

Such poetic moments were rare as the retreating army struggled through the mountains. They crossed into Hunan and reached the Hsiang-Hsiang River. Renewed rain, plus a clever flanking attack, permitted them to capture a floating pontoon bridge before the Hunanese army could destroy it. But the weather cleared before the entire army could cross. In the rear the Nationalist army from Kiangsi was still struggling to catch up, and in front there was but a small group of the Hunanese provincial troops. The bulk of the Hunanese army had rushed north when Ho Lung, in response to a secret message from Chu Teh, broke out of his mountain soviet and raided a Hunan city. Jubilation ran through the marching troops. They anticipated an easy victory. But the clearing clouds brought back the Kuomintang air force.

The planes came in low over the river, flashing down its length with machine guns blazing. Men on the crowded bridge leaped into the muddy yellow water, although most of them could not swim. (The bulk of the Red Army was composed of inland Chinese who came from areas where water was not plentiful). Even so, the dirty river was preferable to the blazing guns firing at them. On the banks, soldiers knelt hastily and fired back with rifles. Machine gun crews, who had their weapons strapped to the backs of the lower-ranking members of their squads, struggled to set up their guns.

The first wave of strafing fighters passed. Because of the high hills on each side of the river, the planes could not turn rapidly. The last of the main columns had crossed the bridge by this time, leaving only the rear guard, numbering some three thousand, on the other bank. Before it could catch up and cross, the planes were back. The center of the bridge sagged as a hail of bullets ripped into the pontoons, and they filled with water.

This time the fighters were followed by a flight of light bombers. The earth shook, and geysers of water shot up as a stick of 300-pound bombs fell across the bridge. The bridge broke in two. As the swift current swept the broken ends downstream, the mooring lines on the left bank gave away and an entire half of the bridge went bobbing down the river. This ruined any chance they might have had of repairing the bridge and bringing the rear guard over.

There is a story that Chu Teh, when he realized that those on the other side were now lost to the main body, climbed up on a bluff where they could see him. He waved at them. Hundreds saw him and waved back. Chu Teh, in contrast to most commanders in both the Red and White armies—or any other army for that matter—was totally democratic. He was a familiar figure wandering constantly through the army camps, talking to men of every rank. Often he would find some soldiers who had found some extra food to supplement their meager rations and would sit down and join them at their meal. He would even, on occasion, help them cook. In fact, his nickname among the soldiers was "the Cook." Years before, when captured by Kuomintang troops, he had escaped execution by convincing the White Army commander that he was only the camp cook.

When Chu Teh waved goodbye, both he and the lost troops knew that the chances of their ever seeing each other again were extremely remote. The lost regiments faded back into the thick growth of cedars that choked the mountains in that part of Hunan, breaking into guerrilla groups to stab at the enemy and run. Eventually many of them were able to get through the enemy lines and join Ho Lung's Fourth Route army.

This was more than those who got across the river could do. At first they were successful, occupying five south Hunan towns, but the masses of troops between them and their goal,

Ho Lung's soviet in north Hunan, were too much. The Revolutionary Military Council, headed by Chou En-lai with Li Te planning the strategy, decided to change the original plan and head for Szechuan province, which bordered on Tibet.

Mao Tse-tung was not a member of the Revolutionary Military Council at that time. General Chu Teh was, and he kept Mao informed of the council's decisions. Mao listened but said little openly. His opinions were well known and had been the reason for his expulsion from the Central Committee.

In the evenings, when no battles were to be fought or night marches made, Mao and Chu Teh often sat together and talked long into the night. Chu placed more dependence on Mao's military opinions than on those of the Central Committee. Committee members knew that their Red Army commander-in-chief was a Maoist. But Chu Teh retained his command because he had the faith of the common soldiers and was as brilliant a field general as China had ever produced.

Throughout the Long March Mao carried a large knapsack on his back. That was his office. The interior of the knapsack was divided into compartments to keep his important papers separated. He worked on these papers, developing his long-range plans, at every stop.

During this time he was being ignored by the Central Committee. He had not been forgiven for his refusal to embrace Stalinism. Despite this rejection by his Party's leaders, Mao Tse-tung had been able—with Chu Teh's military help—to build his Kiangsi soviet into the largest Communist state in China. His soviet was gone now—destroyed largely because the Central Committee's bungling in other parts of China had caused defeats that permitted Chiang Kai-shek to mass the bulk of his troops against the Kiangsi soviet. Now Mao worked alone in the late night, planning his comeback. His papers were spread out on a crudely built table put together by his

"Little Devil" orderlies. Mao was certain that the Central Committee's policies would end in disaster. When that disaster came he intended to be prepared to take full advantage of it. To this end he talked to Chu Teh and some of the other generals who shared Chu Teh's respect for Mao's ability as a military strategist.

The Red Army now turned west into adjoining Kweichow province, which lay between Hunan and their new goal in Szechuan province. Kweichow is wetter than the area they had left. They encountered rain every day. It was cold and they were uncomfortable in the chilly November air, but the rain was welcome, for it slowed the Nationalists' attacks and grounded Chiang Kai-shek's bombers and fighter planes.

Up to this point the retreat had been easy, relatively speaking. Now they suddenly faced a formidable natural barrier giving them the first hint that nature might turn out to be a more devastating enemy than Chiang Kai-shek. The road they were following through the pine- and cedar-choked mountains stopped at a sheer cliff, which towered in the air at nearly a ninety-degree angle. Ages before this, someone had carved handholds and toeholds in the rock face so that human packers could work their way up and down carrying sacks of salt on their backs from Kweichow wells to market in Hunan and Kiangsi.

It was impossible to get the pack animals up the cliff. Yet they could not be abandoned, although much of the heavy equipment they packed was useless on the march, limiting their advance to three miles an hour. Later writers call this a "characteristic mistake."

However, this inconvenience had all been taken into account. If the Red Army had intended to spend the rest of its days as small guerrilla forces, hitting and running, then the criticism would have been justified. They would have been guilty of burdening themselves unnecessarily with useless material. But the basic strategy was different. They intended to form another soviet, and the dismantled arsenal, the printing presses for propaganda, the sewing machines, the turning lathes, and other machine tools were important in establishing an economic unit instead of a group of war camps scattered through the mountains.

Faced with this impassable barrier, they could not carry their supplies forward. Behind them, the Hunan warlord Ho Chien had scorched the earth, burning crops and houses so that the Red Army could not live off the land. Also, Chiang Kai-shek was pushing hard on their rear guard. Then, beyond the mountain, according to Chu Teh's spies, Kweichow and Kuomintang troops were massing for a frontal assault.

While there was a difficult but passable mountain trail around the sheer bluff, the nature of the terrain made it a trap for any military force stupid enough to use it. It wound through deep gorges. The first part would be easy enough, for it was undefended, but the last section would be suicidal for the Red Army. The defending Kweichow troops, sitting on the high bluffs above the invaders, could roll rocks down upon the hapless supply train, block trails with dynamite charges, and blast trapped men from well-placed machine gun emplacements.

Despite their precarious situation, Chu Teh split his forces. The pack animals and supply corps were sent around the gorge trail. About half of the fighting force preceded them. The rest of the soldiers were marched straight up the cliff. An unnamed soldier later wrote an account of that difficult climb. He wrote that the steps up part of the cliff were so far apart that a man could not stretch his legs from one to the other. He had to balance on one, then grasp another with his outstretched hand and pull himself up. Another soldier was quoted by Agnes Smedley as saying, "The mountain was so steep I could see the soles of the man ahead of me. Steps had been carved in the stone face. They were as high as a man's waist."

Loaded as they were with packs containing all their belongings, their weapons and ammunition belts, and their sausage bags of rice, even the strongest soldier found the climb almost beyond his strength. After a while they got above the perpendicular climb, but the narrow, winding ledge was just as dangerous. Political commissars, who were assigned to every unit, ran back and forth, encouraging the falterers, helping those who stumbled, and loudly singing Communist inspirational songs. In this respect none worked harder than Chu Teh. One soldier reported later, "General Chu was everywhere, encouraging everyone. He was never sick. He never faltered, and the blacker things got the more cheerful he became."

By morning it was apparent what Chu Teh had in mind. The mass of the marchers were decoys for the enemy. Sure that the Red Army was heading straight into a death trap, the Kweichow war lord moved his troops to strike the decisive blow. Not only did he have the bulk of the Red Army trapped, he thought, but he also was in a position to capture its treasury. Mao and Chu Teh had a strict rule that nothing was to be taken from peasants without paying for it. To this end they carried large amounts of Kuomintang money taken from rich landowners, and also several mule-loads of silver.

But as the Kweichow troops moved in to strike the marchers in the gorge trap, they were suddenly hit from the rear in a surprise attack by Chu Teh's troops, who had climbed the sheer cliff. The opium-soaked mercenary Kweichow provincial troops (notorious for their drug addiction) faltered, and then fled. Better trained and disciplined Kuomintang troops were rushed in for reinforcements, but they were insufficient to stop the Red Army.

Chu Teh recombined his split forces and smashed through the opposition. They headed for central Kweichow, whose capital, Chungking, the Revolutionary Military Council had selected as their next goal. They hoped that booty in military arms they would find there, plus the money they expected to extract from wealthy merchants and landowners, would replenish their dwindling resources.

The selection of Chungking as the military target proved to be another error. However, it raised their spirits. They plunged ahead, not knowing that the real torment of the Long March had not yet begun.

2

The Seeds of Revolution

The Long March may have started in Kiangsi in October 1934, but its real beginning lies deep in Chinese history. Feudalism had been the law of the land since the first records were kept. During all those centuries, China was an agrarian nation primarily, and most of the farmers were destitute tenants tilling the soil for absentee landlords.

Under such conditions the peasant class was saddled with rents that sometimes took as much as seventy per cent of their crops. Then there was a measure that was seized by the tax collector, leaving the farmer with scarcely enough to feed his family for a year, even in good times. But good times came rarely. Floods, locusts, pestilence and droughts added to his woes and miseries.

Periodically things got so bad that the people broke out in revolt. Sometimes the revolts were strong enough to topple dynasties, but more often they were put down after mass executions. Peasant revolts rarely amounted to anything permanent, because they did not have proper leadership or strong motivation. The peasant was interested only in alleviating a harsh condition. He had no knowledge of government itself. If his taxes and rents were eased, that was the height of his ambition.

In later years, when China began to industrialize, things were no better for those who toiled in the factories. Children as young as eight years old worked sixteen hours a day and were paid in pennies.

Such intolerable conditions were fertile ground for revolution, but nothing came of it except occasional political strife aimed at overthrowing the Manchu government that seized China from the Ming dynasty in 1644 A.D. The first great attempt at revolution began in 1848, led by a strange man named Hung Hsui-chuan. Hung appears in history as a curious religious fanatic whose struggles to build an empire read almost like an outline for what Mao Tse-tung and Chu Teh accomplished eighty years later.

Hung, distraught because of repeated failures to pass the difficult government civil service examinations, had a strange vision. He dreamed that an angel came from heaven and cut open Hung's stomach. The angel then removed Hung's heart and other organs and replaced them with new ones brought down from Heaven. This change qualified Hung as a Prince of Heaven. He then developed a personal philosophy based partly on his own peculiar interpretation of Christianity and set out to make China his personal kingdom on earth.

Surprisingly, Hung attracted thousands of converts, especially among the hard-pressed peasants. He was soon able to start guerrilla warfare against the imperial Manchu army. His revolt was making small progress when peasants in Kwangsi province, hard hit by famine, revolted against the imperial tax collectors in 1850. The tax revolt was quickly suppressed, but thousands of the rebels joined Hung's liberation army. The jubilant religious fanatic then announced that he was forming a new dynasty destined to rule all China. He called it *Taiping Tienkuo* or Heavenly Kingdom of Great Peace. His revolt became known as the Taiping Rebellion.

Hung teamed with a military genius named Chu Kiu-tao, who organized the Taiping army—said to number 30,000,000 at one time—along surprisingly modern and efficient lines. In many ways Chu's policies antedated those of Mao and Chu Teh. One of these was an absolute prohibition of looting by his soldiers. They were required to pay for anything taken from the people. Opium smoking was abolished, and women were given equal treatment with men. Many of his reforms, relating to communal life, directly anticipated Communism, although Chu Kiu-tao formed his ideas before Karl Marx and Friedrich Engels issued their *Communist Manifesto* in 1848.

The Taiping Rebellion gained enormous strength after Chu's no-loot policy convinced the lower classes that the Taipings were on the side of the common people. By 1853 Hung and Chu controlled a large section of central China and launched an attack on the important Yangtze city of Nanking. Twenty thousand defending Manchus were slaughtered, and the army pressed on for an attack on the Manchu capital in Peking.

The Peking attack failed, but the Taipings continued to enlarge their holdings in south China during the next seven years. The strength of the Taiping Rebellion and its effect on Western trade alarmed foreign nations, whose China traders complained that a total Taiping victory would hurt or possibly destroy the rich economic concessions they had in China.

After this, Western nations began to support the Manchus. Two adventurers, an American named Frederick Townsend Ward, and an Englishman called "Chinese" Gordon, led the Manchu army to battle, achieving decisive victories over the

Taipings in 1863. By that time Townsend Ward had been killed. Chinese Gordon resigned in anger when the Manchus killed four Taiping princes who came to bargain under a flag of truce. The 1863 campaign broke the power of the Taiping army, but fighting continued for the next eighteen months. In 1865 the great Manchu general Tseng Kuo-fan captured the Taiping capital at Nanking. Hung, the Prince of Heaven, committed suicide, and members of his family were slaughtered, along with thousands of the Taiping court. (The Communistic policies Hung instituted for Taiping China had not prevented that Prince of Heaven from living like the traditional Chinese emperor.)

The remnants of the Taiping army, under Taiping Prince Shih Ta-kai, fled into western China just as the Kiangsi soviet fled on their Long March sixty-nine years later. The Taipings' Long March ended on the brink of the Tatu River gorge, where they were all slaughtered by Tseng Kuo-fan.

By a coincidence of history the Kiangsi Communists were also headed toward Tatu Gorge, although they did not know it when they marched through Kweichow—and Chiang Kai-shek, the man pursuing them, had taken Tseng Kuo-fan as his hero when Chiang was a young man studying military tactics. However—unfortunate for a complete replay of history—Mao Tse-tung and Chu Teh also had studied the Taiping Rebellion.

The next historic attempt at rebellion had not been directed against the government but actually had had government secret support. This was the Boxer Rebellion of 1900, when fanatics attempted to drive foreigners from China. China's experience with Western nations had been devastating throughout the nineteenth century. She had twice been at war with England, losing badly each time. France had seized Indo-China. Russia had encroached on Manchuria, and in 1895—as a result of the Sino-Japanese war—China had lost

Taiwan and Korea. These territorial losses, coupled with unqual trade treaties forced upon China by the victors, had fostered the hatred that sparked the Boxer Rebellion. The Boxers were crushed by foreign intervention (which included the U.S. Marines and some Army units), but the Boxer spirit found expression among bitter young Chinese who felt that their country's hope for survival lay in overthrowing the ineffectual Manchu government. They hoped to build in its place a government strong enough to resist a foreign dismemberment of China.

Among these young men was a born rebel named Sun Wen, whom the Western world came to know under the name of Sun Yat-sen. Sun was such a rebel as a child that his exasperated father shipped the boy to Hawaii, where it was hoped his elder brother could control him. The brother had no success in taming Sun either, however. He soon sent the boy back to China. Sun spent six months in his native village in Kwantung before he was banished for preaching against the old gods of China.

In the nomadic years that followed, Sun Yat-sen studied the history of foreign aggression in China and developed into an ardent revolutionist. He also studied medicine in Hong Kong because he had learned that the Chinese people respected doctors and listened to them. He thought the doctor title would aid him in organizing revolts.

He staged his first revolt in 1895, attempting to seize Canton. The uprising failed, and Sun fled first to the United States and then to London. Here the long arm of the vengeful Empress Dowager of China caught up with Sun. He was walking down a London Street when two Chinese suddenly came up behind him. Sun tried to run, but they forced him to cross the street, where they dragged him into the Chinese legation. They planned to smuggle their captive back to China for execution.

Fortunately for Sun, his old medical instructor from Hong Kong, Sir James Cantlie, was in London. Sun bribed a servant to take Sir James a note. When the British government claimed that it could do nothing about the kidnapping, Sir James appealed to the newspapers, which broadcast the situation. An angry British mob surrounded the Chinese legation, and the ambassador hurriedly ordered Sun's release.

After leaving London, Sun Yat-sen staged a series of unsuccessful revolts before a nation-wide revolution finally did break out in 1911. By February, 1912, the Manchu government abdicated. Sun Yat-sen was hailed as China's George Washington.

His triumph, however, was short lived. The country split into a dozen political units with warlords in control of the provinces. Sun succeeded in organizing a Nationalist government only in the area about Canton.

In 1921 the political situation was complicated still more by the formation of the Chinese Communist Party. Twelve men, including Mao Tse-tung, had met secretly in a girl's school in Shanghai to start the party. Stalin, through the "Comintern"—Communist International—ordered the new party to work closely with Dr. Sun's Kuomintang party. Sun believed that American democracy was unsuited to China's problems and he wanted a modified form of Marxism. This was not the basic reason for Stalin's order, however. The Russian dictator was concerned about possible Western Nations' intervention in China to protect their trade interests. He expected Britain at least to send troops into China if the disorder continued. With this possibility facing them, Stalin wanted the two Chinese Communist-sympathizing groups to work together despite some basic differences. These differences could be eliminated later by purges in the Russian manner. While Stalin did not approve of all the policies of Dr. Sun and the Kuomintang, he was just as suspicious of Mao

Tse-tung, whose basic ideas were at odds with Russian Marxist objectives.

As envisioned by Karl Marx, Communism started with a dictatorship of the working class. Marx had reviewed all previous revolutions and had come to the conclusion that peasants do not make good revolutionaries. As a result of his studies, he advocated organizing the working classes of the cities. According to his plan, the capitalists would be wiped out as a ruling class and the peasant class would be gathered in communes to act as the bread basket for the dictatorship of the workers.

Mao Tse-tung disagreed. He distrusted the working class and felt that it represented too small a section of China. In highly industrialized countries like Germany, England and the United States, there were enough big-city working class people to mount a revolution, but not in China. Mao's arguments, forcifully put to the Central Committee of the Chinese Communist Party, were that the Chinese peasantry would support a truly revolutionary force, and that the Communist Party could not hope to win its revolution unless it gained massive support.

Sun Yat-sen died in 1925 and was succeeded by Chiang Kai-shek. Chiang had been influenced by Dr. Sun while still in his teens. Later, Chiang had gone to Russia for study and advanced training in military tactics. He had returned to China to head the Whampoa Military Academy of the Chinese Nationalist Army.

Some of the ablest generals in both the Kuomintang and Communist armies were Whampoa graduates. In fact, a group of Chiang's former students formed the "Whampoa clique," which, together with the "28 Bolsheviks," dominated the Central Committee of the Chinese Communist party. The "Bolsheviks" were twenty-eight young men who had trained in Russia and returned to China. Both the Bolsheviks and the

Whampoa clique strongly supported the Stalinists against the Maoists, who wanted to organize the peasants.

In 1926 Chiang led the Nationalist Army in an invasion of north China. His object was to break the power of the provincial warlords and bring the country under Nationalist control. At first he won easy victories. The first major one was the capture of Wuhan. Wuhan is an industrial area, rather than a city, and takes in the cities of Hankow, Wuchang and Hangyang.

While Chiang pushed on north to capture Nanking and Shanghai, the Nationalist governmant moved its headquarters from Canton to Wuhan. Immediately the members began plotting against their commander-in-chief. It appeared that Chiang would succeed in uniting China, and they feared he would set up a dictatorship. They could not depose him, since they needed him as a soldier. So, instead, they reorganized the military command structure, making all of the Nationalist generals equal in status. This made Chiang just another field commander instead of commander-in-chief.

Chiang blamed the Communists for his demotion, and on April 12, 1927, he attacked left-wing forces in Shanghai, slaughtering thousands. Then, two days after the blood bath in Shanghai, Chiang rushed to pull a similar coup in Canton. That was followed by an announcement by Chiang on April 24 proclaiming a new Nationalist Government with headquarters at Nanking. The stunned Wuhan government tried to preserve its identity by continued collaboration with the Chinese Communist Party, but Stalin insisted on supporting Chiang. The Wuhan government continued in existence until September, 1927, when it dissolved.

Chiang then did an about-face in order to avoid trouble between the two Nationalist groups. He withdrew from the presidency of the New Nationalist Kuomintang, permitting Wang Ching-wei, the president of the old Nationalist group, to assume the Kuomintang leadership in name. However, Chiang, although he left for Japan, kept tight control of the army. As soon as conditions warranted, he returned to China and ousted Wang, whom everyone had considered Sun Yat-sen's chosen heir. By the end of 1928 Chiang had defeated the last of the northern warlords and headed the recognized government of China.

One of the mysteries of international politics is what Stalin had in mind when he backed Chiang Kai-shek over the Chinese Communist Party. Perhaps he had little faith in the party leaders but believed that Chiang, who had been trained in Moscow, was only putting up an anti-Communist front, as Castro of Cuba would do later, and would return to the fold once his power was consolidated. In any event, Stalin was wrong.

While this was going on, Mao Tse-tung was ignoring Comintern orders to cooperate with Chiang Kai-shek. He also went against the policy of the Chinese Communist Party. He began organizing peasant guerrilla groups and launched the "Autumn Harvest Uprising," a peasant revolt, in late August, 1927, in defiance of Stalin's order to cooperate with Chiang Kai-shek.

The revolt was doomed from the start. The peasant guerrillas were too poorly trained to fight the experienced Kuomintang troops. Mao managed to escape with about a thousand men. He retreated to Chingkanshan, a rugged mountain stronghold on the border of Kiangsi and Hunan. In a short time he was joined by General Chu Teh, who was also fleeing from a disastrous battle with the Kuomintang. Mao and Chu Teh joined forces and began building what later became the Kiangsi soviet, a Communist republic inside China.

Mao's Autumn Harvest Uprising was important in Chiang's decision whether to turn to the East or the West for support. He chose the West for a number of reasons. First of all, he felt that he could not trust the Communists. Mao's uprising in defiance of Stalin's cooperation order had proved that. Also many of his Kuomintang officers were middle-class landowners. They were afraid that Communist control would sweep away private ownership. Since Chiang depended upon them to support his power, he could not ignore their wishes.

Also, Chiang had married Soong Mei-ling in 1927. This alliance with the rich and powerful Soong family made Chiang the brother-in-law of a rich banker named H. H. Kung, who claimed direct descent from Confucius. Kung and T. V. Soong, Chiang's other new brother-in-law, were staunch capitalists and both viewed Communism as a personal threat. They brought heavy pressure on Chiang to fight it.

Chiang also had to consider foreign sentiment, for Western governments would fight to protect their trade. Foreign traders were entrenched in China's port cities. By the very nature of their business, they were anti-Communist. China had suffered some bitter and bloody defeats by trying to interfere with these foreign traders.

On the other side, Chiang Kai-shek had Stalin's support. But this took the form of advisers and orders from the Comintern. Actually, very little in the way of armaments and supplies came from Russia under Stalin. The Comintern was interested in exporting revolution, but it expected that revolution to be self-supporting. (In later years, Chu Teh said that he had never received as much as a single gun from the Russians. All his battles were fought with materiel captured from the Kuomintang army.)

Chiang made his decision and turned violently against the Chinese Communist Party. He immediately launched on "extermination campaign" against what he termed the "Red bandits." One of his first targets was Chingkanshan, where Mao and Chu Teh had taken refuge. That wild volcanic peak had been a bandit hideout for centuries and was impregnable.

Chiang surrounded the mountain and eventually starved the defenders out. However, Chu Teh and Mao managed to break through the Kuomintang lines and escaped into Kiangsi, where they set up a new soviet. As the years passed, Chiang mounted a second, a third, and a fourth extermination campaign.

The fortunes of Mao and Chu Teh went up and down, but they gradually expanded their territory until they controlled a large area on the Kiangsi-Fukien border, centering on Juichin. The soviet grew so large that Mao declared a Communist republic, with himself as President of the Provisional Central Committee of the Kiangsi Soviet.

Other soviets were established by Red generals in other sections, but Mao's Kiangsi republic was the largest and the most successful. Much of Mao's success was based upon his belief that the Communist revolution would not succeed without using a peasant base. The Chinese Communist Party still was attempting to capture large cities and build its revolution on a base of urban working class people.

In furthering Mao's policy of cultivating the peasants, Chu Teh followed almost exactly the principles laid down by the other General Chu who had won so many victories for the Taiping Rebellion. Nothing was ever taken from the peasants that was not paid for. Rules of conduct were drawn up and any soldier who violated them was severely punished.

Among the rules were such things as: "Be courteous to people and help them. Return all borrowed articles. Replace any articles you damage. Be honest in all transactions with the people. Pay for all articles purchased."

According to Robert Goldston, "These rules were a revolution in Chinese military conduct. For thousands of years the soldier had been dreaded and hated by the peasant . . . But here was a new kind of army—an army that helped the peasants plant their grain and helped them harvest it; an army that did not rob . . . ."

The political situation became even more confused in 1931 when the Japanese invaded the Chinese province of Manchuria, which contained the largest part of China's industry. Chiang appealed to the United States and Great Britain for help, but both were sunk in an economic depression and neither country wanted to become embroiled in a foreign war. Chiang then appealed to the League of Nations. This proved futile. None of the members wanted to challenge Japan at that time. Chiang, in turn, did not want to fight the Japanese, for he felt that the Communists were a greater enemy. So he left Chang Hsueh-liang, the warlord of Manchuria, to handle the invaders as best he could, with Chiang giving only token assistance.

Chiang assembled an army of a million men during the next two years. Again he ignored the Japanese invaders in Manchuria. Instead he launched his Fifth Red Bandit Extermination Campaign. This time he had expert German advice. As his successes mounted, the Communist Party's Central Committee fled to Kiangsi, seeking the protection of Chu Teh's demonstrated military ability.

Chiang's German-built ring of steel gradually squeezed in on the Kiangsi soviet. Mao and Chu, seeing their Communist state tottering toward destruction, agreed with the Central Committee's plan to abandon Kiangsi, and the Long March started.

In abandoning Kiangsi they were following the basic military tactics that governed all of Mao Tse-tung's and Chu Teh's fighting. According to what Chu Teh told Agnes Smedley (repeated by numerous writers who neglected to give their source), these tactical principles were as follows:

- When the enemy advances, we retreat.
- When the enemy halts, we harrass.
- When the enemy retreats, we pursue.
- When the enemy tries to avoid battle, we attack.

The enemy was now advancing, and the First Route Red Army began to retreat. In many ways the march across Kiangsi, the lower corner of Hunan, and into Kweichow had been a highly successful military maneuver. Unfortunately, the losses in men and materiel had been so high that the Red Army was being bled to death. Its successes in battle were costing too much.

The Revolutionary Military Council was not disheartened, however. They had failed to break through into Hunan to join with Ho Lung's army in the northern part of the province, but they felt that the notoriously poor fighting spirit of the Kweichow provincial troops would offer little opposition. They felt the Red Army could slice through them easily and make for a small soviet in the northern section of Szechuan. Here they hoped to combine, draw refugees from other defeated soviets, and rebuild for a counterattack, which they hoped would destroy Chiang Kai-shek entirely.

Mao Tse-tung, on the outside of the Military Council, did not agree. He was sure that the Military Council's policy was leading them to destruction. He continued to hunch over his maps and make plans at each stop, for he was certain that the day was coming when those plans would save the Red Army from destruction.

And he was right.

3

🐚

Showdown At Tsunyi

A battle is such a confused mess that no one ever really knows later what actually happened. Those who took part are generally the most ignorant of the overall picture. They have seen individually only a small part of the vast maneuvering that has taken place. Even the general, sitting in his head-quarters pouring over his maps, knows only the final results and can speak only of mass movements of units. The tens of thousands of small pieces that went into the victory or defeat are lost in the stress and confusion of killing or being killed, so it is difficult to reconstruct a battle.

One participant will tell you that it was the hardest-fought battle in history. Another will claim he never had it so easy. Both probably are right. Reporters who talked with Chu Teh often complained that the great general became confused when talking of the battles of the Long March, often getting them out of chronology and sometimes even forgetting some he fought. As a result, when we come to the question of what was the hardest time the refugees had on the Long March, we must depend upon personal and conflicting views. However, there seems to be general agreement that the worst fighting encountered was in Kweichow and Szechuan. Chou En-lai has said so, and General Lo Ping-hui strongly agrees on the bitterness of Kweichow fighting.

In contrast to the other leaders—Chu Teh excepted—General Lo was a jovial man. He was said to be the possessor of the biggest stomach in the entire Communist army. Like Chu Teh, Lo Ping-hui spent most of his time wandering among his troops. He was not a headquarters fighter but a man who was happiest when he was in the middle of a battle.

Once, Lo was criticized for keeping too close to the front line. He replied that he could not give orders unless he knew what was going on. This remark did not endear him to the Revolutionary Military Council, who interpreted it as a sly dig at their interference with field commanders.

Lo was picked by Chu Teh to command the rear-guard elements of the Long March because of his great reputation as a hard-fighting, wily commander who constantly kept his enemy off-balance with shifting tactics, tricks and surprises.

Most of those who have left accounts of the Long March give the impression that troop morale was always high. Lo Ping-hui told a different story. He said that troop morale was bad as the First Front Red Army staggered out of Hunan and moved into Kweichow province. The soldiers had been marching for two months, fighting every day as they struggled through almost constant rain and mud. They had won most of their battles but lost nearly 15,000 men while doing it.

To make matters worse, there was growing dissension between members of the Revolutionary Military Council and the field commanders regarding basic strategy. Mao Tse-tung kept quiet, but Chu Teh was among the most vocal in the strategy meeting of the Council. Lo Ping-hui also was silent, but it was plain that neither he nor Lin Piao, a brilliant general, were happy with things as they stood. It appeared from the direction the First Front Red Army was taking now that their goals had been shifted to an attack on Chunking. That was in line with the basic party tactic of trying to capture large cities where the working classes could be organized. Chu Teh, taking his cue from Mao, insisted that that approach had always failed and would fail again.

One of the natural obstacles in the road to Chungking was the Wu River. Later, General Lo told Nym Wales that the Wu was "my most critical experience during the Long March."

However, the Wu was not as deep, swift or dangerous to cross as the Yangtze, which lay directly ahead. Lo's trouble came when the Red Army suddenly found itself boxed in by four enemy armies coming from different directions. Nationalist armies from Szechuan, Kweichow and Hunan hit them from three sides. The pursuing army from Kiangsi, under the personal direction of Chiang Kai-shek, was behind them, cutting off any possibility of retreat along the way they had come.

The Revolutionary Military Council, following the strategy mapped by the German Li Te (the Chinese name for Otto Braun), drove on toward Chungking. Here they hoped to capture the city, set up a soviet, and stand off the Nationalists with positional warfare. As they advanced toward Chungking, the First Front Army captured a major bridge across the Wu. Then, when the enemy closed in, the Council radioed General Lo that it was imperative to blow up the bridge to prevent pursuit by Chiang's Kuomintang troops.

Lo was far in the rear, fighting a rearguard action. His radio was out of commission and he did not receive the message until six o'clock in the evening. The bridge was scheduled to be blown up at nine the next morning. Lo was then sixty-five miles south of the river with fifteen hundred men who were slowing the advance of a large body of reinforcements pushing up from the south to join Chiang Kai-shek's divisions.

When he received word that the bridge would be destroyed and his troops would be marooned on the south side of the Wu if he could not reach the bridge in time, General Lo had just completed one of his typically tricky maneuvers. He had moved forward until scouts almost made contact with the advancing Kuomintang vanguard, which outnumbered his 1,500 men thirty-five to one.

Then he had suddenly retreated, splitting his force into groups that took possession of two mountains directly in front of the advancing Kuomintang army. Lo had then set his soldiers to marching in circles around the mountains' side. He was careful to order that they should try to keep mostly undercover but should cross clearings where they would be visible to the enemy.

The idea of this maneuver was to trick the Kuomintang into believing they faced a much larger force than Lo actually had. The tactic can be compared to that of a theatrical director who creates the impression of a mob by having his cast cross the stage, circle around behind the scenery and cross the stage time and again to give an impression of double, triple or quadruple the number of actors he has.

Lo had carried his conception still further. When Kuomintang planes scouted the mountains, he had kept considerable men and materiel in the open. This had caused Nationalist photographic interpreters to report that the Red Army was so large that all of it could not be hidden under the cedar and pine trees that covered the mountains.

As a result of these tricks, the Kuomintang forces were not eager to launch an immediate attack. They had halted, and the general had radioed to the rear for additional reinforcements. He claimed that he had contacted the main body of the First Front Red Army.

Lo had then split his force into three parts. He had kept one third on the mountains, where they could be seen by the enemy. The remaining two thirds were broken into small guerrilla units, who slipped around and began harrassing the enemy's flanks. The fighting was light, but it did serve to confuse the Nationalist commanders. It was not Lo's purpose to join in a big fight. He had only wanted to delay the enemy troops until Chu Teh broke through the battle line being thrown up in the front of the main First Front Red Army by the warlord of Szechuan. This he had been able to do for two days.

At that point Lo received the radio call that Chu Teh would be forced to blow up the Wu River bridge not later than nine the next day to prevent Chiang's other force from crossing behind the Red Army. This force was coming from Hunan.

Lo wheeled his men and started a desperate forced march to reach the Wu before the bridge was demolished. He understood why Chu Teh could not wait longer than nine o'clock for them to arrive. If the Hunan troops got across the Wu, the main body of the Red Army would be caught in a pincers attack between the Hunan and the Szechuan armies.

The land Lo had to march over was so rugged that Kweichow natives had a local saying: "There is no level ground more than a mile long."

Lo put it a different way. He said, "We had to march five miles up and down in order to advance one mile in a straight line!" There were hundreds of streams of different width and depths, which cut through the high hills to slow their passage. And the constant up and down climbs sapped the troops' strength.

Lo's problem was to cover sixty-five miles in fifteen hours. The rugged terrain made that difficult, but the Communist general also had to avoid being caught between the army that was pursuing him and the Hunan forces who were advancing toward the Wu bridge from the east. In running away from the force behind, he was moving directly toward the force from Hunan, and there was nothing he could do about it. There was absolutely no place he could cross the Wu except at the bridge. This situation was what Lo called "my most critical experience of the entire Long March."

By nine o'clock the next morning, after marching all night, they were still nine miles from the Wu. Demolition squads from Lin Piao's division dynamited the bridge on schedule. Lo Ping-hui was trapped.

He radioed for instructions and received this message in reply:"Plan your strategy according to the immediate situation." The "immediate situation" was desperate. The bulk of Lo's men, coming from upland China, could not swim. Their sausage bags were empty of rice, and the enemy was pressing on them from two directions.

An hour later he discovered that Kweichow provincial troops were moving in from a third direction. Lo now estimated that his meager 1,500 troops faced odds not less than fifty-to-one. He called a hasty council of war with his officers. They realized as well as Lo Ping-hui did that the situation was the worst they had faced since starting the Long March.

No one had any suggestions. They were trapped. Lo was left with three alternatives. One was to surrender—but this was worse than fighting to the death of the last man, since everyone from Lo himself to the last private in the rear rank could then expect execution at the hands of the vengeful provincial troops. The second alternative, often taken by Red Army units cut off from their main force, was to disband into small guerrilla squads and settle in the local area to continue fighting as best they could.

Lo's third choice was to try to confuse the enemy so that his beleaguered forces might find a loophole to slip through. Lo had often done this in the past, but never against such odds as he faced now. However, he rejected the idea of disbanding his army and letting them escape as best they could.

Instead, he wheeled to the left and crossed a small river that was shallow enough for his nonswimming troops to wade. His spies told him that the enemy facing him here were Szechuan troops, who were all opium-smoking mercenaries. They had little will to fight, and they fell back in confusion when Lo attacked.

Instead of rushing into the breach that left—which might have closed around him if the Szechuan officers could have succeeded in rallying their soldiers—Lo ordered his buglers to sound retreat. His men turned and charged back across the river the way they had come. The Nationalist general who had been pursuing them had not expected this maneuver. He and his men were unprepared to face the Reds when Lo reversed his charge and advanced toward them.

The resulting battle was one of wild confusion, which aided Lo. The Nationalists pulled back to regroup, leaving a large number of dead. Lo lost about a hundred men. He now turned again, hitting a force that attacked his flank. Then he broke his army into guerrilla bands numbering from fifty to one hundred men each. They began to attack the enemy with swift hit-and-run stabs that added to the confusion in the Kuomintang army. They would move in at night, strike hard, and fade back to another position. The enemy never knew for sure where they were or how large a force they faced.

The Nationalists—except for the Szechuan regiments—fought hard. Lo lost another hundred men. While he had won every fight so far, the victories were bleeding him to death. He was also out of food and had no place there in the hills where he could forage for more. Ammunition was running low. He managed to capture a Nationalist supply company but got few munitions.

When Lo had split his troops into guerrilla bands, he had given orders to reassemble at a selected point before dawn. When the weary fighters staggered in, Lo gave them no rest. He marched them back to a mountain free from Kuomintang soldiers. A small force was sent up the slope, where they could be seen by the enemy when the sun finally came up. The rest of the force circled the base of the mountain, taking care to keep under cover. Lo was repeating his previous trick.

The Kuomintang general set out in pursuit of the mountain troops he could see. This permitted Lo to march the main body of his soldiers out of immediate danger.

When Lo sent the diversionary force up the mountain, he gave them the same orders he had received from the Council: "Plan your strategy according to the immediate situation." Red Army leaders had to be self-sufficient if they expected to survive. By some miracle the bulk of the diversionary company maneuvered around and evaded the enemy. All but seven eventually rejoined Lo's main group.

Lo now made a wide circle that took him back to the Wu River. There was no place to ford. So he moved up the banks of the stream until he was suddenly cut off by four enemy regiments. There was no way to retreat. They had to stand and fight against four-to-one odds. Once again, Lo had to make a decision whether to disband into permanent guerrilla bands or to hope for some break that would permit them to stay together.

Then he made contact with some farmers who were friendly to the Communists. Their help made him decide to keep fighting. He tried to avoid battle but was trapped and had an all-day fight before he broke loose. They escaped but left three hundred more dead behind them.

Surprisingly, the low morale Lo complained of earlier had vanished, principally because of the soldiers' growing belief in the invincibility of their commander. However, Lo's clever propaganda had as much to do with their change of spirit as anything else.

"During those days at the Wu-kiang, I used to make speeches to my men," Lo later told Nym Wales. "I told them, 'We are like a monkey playing with a cow in a narrow alley. The big, stupid enemy can't move fast. We make him look silly with our clever tricks. We are fighting a glorious war for liberty. We cannot be stopped by a stupid cow in our path!'"

After this, Lo kept edging back to the river, where he hoped to put into effect a daring plan that would either get them across the Wu or end in total destruction of his forces. It was sheer desperation that drove him to this extreme. While his troops held back the enemy, friendly Kweichowese gathered everything that could float—logs, planks, tree limbs, brush, and debris from the destroyed Wu bridge. The wood was tied into improvised rafts, and men piled on them until they were awash. Others waded out into the river and clung to the sides to keep afloat while the rafts were being towed to the opposite bank by farmers who swam ahead with ropes over their shoulders.

As soon as they got close enough to the opposite shore for the soldiers' feet to touch the river bed, the rafts were unloaded and returned for another load.

On one trip, the rope binding holding a raft together broke, probably from the strain of overloading. The soldiers were dumped in the water. Some managed to grab pieces of floating wood to keep themselves afloat. The Kweichow farmers came to the rescue of others, but three soldiers drowned.

By dawn, Lo had his entire force—now numbering only about eight hundred—across the Wu. They were all near exhaustion, but Lo refused them a rest. It was early January, 1935, the coldest month of the year in Kweichow. The area was subtropical, but at that time of the season the temperature

fell to about 40 degrees at night, which is extremely chilly for
men in wet clothing. Lo gave them just enough time to strip
naked and wring the water out of their garments. The first
ones over built a few fires and partially dried their clothes.
The later ones could do nothing but climb out of the river and
start walking to keep warm.

Now, with the river between them and their pursuers, Lo's
group staggered north to rejoin the main force of the First
Front Red Army.

The new Communist target was Tsunyi, the second-largest
city in Kweichow. It was situated between Kweiyang, the
capital, and Chungking, which is across the Yangtze River in
Szechuan. From Tsunyi the Reds hoped to mount an attack on
Chungking. The Fourth Front Red Army under Chang Kuo-
tao had a soviet in north Szechuan. The Central Committee
felt that if the First and Fourth Front armies could combine,
they could hold Chungking in the face of any Nationalist attacks. They could then carve out a new Communist republic
along the lines of the one Mao and Chu Teh had built in
Kiangsi.

Mao told Chu Teh that this was a fatal error. A march
directly north toward Chungking betrayed the Communist
intent. Chiang Kai-shek would be able to mass his troops to
protect the Szechuan city. The Red Army had won their battles so far on the Long March because the enemy had never
been able to determine just where the Reds would move next.
This had forced Chiang to keep his forces broken down into
various units to protect widely scattered points and possible
objectives.

Now their movement had advertised the fact that the Red
Army was bring committed to a frontal attack on Chungking.
That meant positional warfare, which Mao had always argued
against. The Red Army had too few numbers to stand and slug
it out with the enemy. Their strength lay in hit-and-run guerrilla tactics.

Mao's advice was ignored. The Red Army pushed on and took Tsunyi without great difficulty. They then moved toward Chungking and discovered that Mao had been right. Chiang had massed such formidable forces in front of them that it was impossible to cross the Yangtze River in the face of such strong opposition.

After an indecisive battle, the Red Army fell back and re-captured Tsunyi. Here they stopped to rest and reconsider their position. Chiang was regrouping after the Yangtze River battle and was not ready to attack the Red Army at Tsunyi yet. He telegraphed his various commanders: "The fate of the nation and the Kuomintang Party depends upon bottling the Reds up south of the Yangtze."

Another reason for Chiang's delay in pressing a new attack was that he wanted fighting to continue in Kweichow and Yunnan. The warlords of those areas had never submitted to Chiang's control. They agreed to aid him against the Red Army for their own protection but continued to operate as in-dependent governments. Chiang hoped that continued fighting in those two provinces would so weaken the warlords of Kweichow and Yunnan that Chiang could easily defeat them after the Red Army was destroyed. Then the two provinces could be annexed to the Nationalist-controlled areas.

While Chiang prepared for a new battle and plotted against his allies, the Chinese Communist Party was locked in a battle of its own. The Communists' military position was desperate. They could not advance. It was impossible to make the difficult Yangtze River crossing. Nor could they retreat. The Red Army had no way of supplying itself, except by buying food from the peasants and capturing munitions from the enemy. Both of those sources were just about exhausted.

A meeting of the Central Committee was called. It was one of the most fateful meetings of modern times. It was im-portant because it permitted the Red Army to escape defeat and go on to final victory. It also marked the rise of Mao Tse-tung to undisputed party control.

As is the case with many decisive events in history, the Tsunyi meeting's importance passed unnoticed at the time. Even today, it is not being given its proper credit in the story of the rise of Red China. In his famous book *Red Star Over China* Edgar Snow does not mention the Tsunyi conference. Robert Payne gives it only a sketchy page and a half in his biography of Mao Tse-tung. Agnes Smedley, in her biography of Chu Teh, *The Great Road,* does not mention it. Robert Goldston, in *The Rise of Red China*, says only, "There [in Tsunyi] in January of 1935, a conference of the Central Committee of the Chinese Communist Party acknowledged Mao Tse-tung as its leader. Mao became Chairman of the Central Committee, while those whose advice had led to disasters of the previous years stepped down and were replaced by Mao's followers. But Tsunyi was only a stopover on the continuing retreat."

Tsunyi was more than a stopover. At that point, despite the military victories its forces had won, the Red Army was in bad shape. It had lost a third of the soldiers who had marched out of Kiangsi. It was now surrounded by the enemy and in danger of being forced to retreat into Tibet, where its soldiers would starve in the barren highlands.

The Central Committee's strategy had been wrong. It had been trying to capture big cities instead of building up popular support among the peasants and thus creating a base of support for launching a total attack at a later time. The Red Army units were becoming involved in formal positional warfare instead of relying on the guerrilla tactics of which they were masters.

It was clear to all the military commanders that the Red Army could not hold out much longer unless things changed. So, while the Army's political commissars held mass meetings to indoctrinate local peasants and recruit Communist sympathizers and new soldiers, Mao demanded a meeting of the Central Committee to consider strategy and the problems of the immediate future.

For Mao and his opponents in the Party this meeting was a classic example of what Shakespeare wrote in *Julius Caesar*:

> *There is a tide in the affairs of men*
> *Which taken at the flood, leads on to fortune;*
> *Omitted, all the voyages of their life*
> *Is bound in shallows and in misery.*

Members of the Central Committee and the Revolutionary Military Council knew what to expect when Mao demanded the meeting. Mao's view were well known. However, the 28 Bolsheviks and the Whampoa Clique were unable to stop Mao's bid for control; too many mistakes had been made. The military situation was so desperate that Mao got the full backing of a majority of the Red Army's generals and senior commanders.

In addition, Lin Piao broke with the Whampoa Clique and joined the Maoists. Lin, who was considered to be a military tactical genius, recognized the soundness of Mao's basic strategy. (Years later Lin masterminded the Red Chinese intervention in Korea. Eventually, he was to be killed in an airplane crash while fleeing from Red China after being accused of trying to assassinate Mao in order to make himself a military dictator.)

Very little has ever been revealed about what happened at the Tsunyi conference. What has come to light indicates that Mao strongly condemned the conduct of the march up to that point. He accused Li Te of poor strategy for moving in a straight line so that Chiang Kai-shek could anticipate their route. As a result of this poor policy, massed armies were confronting them. Li Te strongly resisted any change in strategy, but when most of the generals supported Mao, Po Ku, secretary of the Chinese Communist Party, resigned. Po Ku had been Li Te's strongest supporter and had acted as interpreter for the German strategist who had taken a Chinese name.

In the reshuffling of offices, Mao was elected chairman of the CCP and Chang Wen-thien took Po Ku's place as party secretary. Teng Fa was dropped as head of the dread secret police who sought out party deviation among the members. At Mao's insistence that post was not refilled.

Mao also replaced Chou En-Lai as chairman of the Military Council. Chou remained on the Council, but in a subordinate position to Mao, who thus emerged from the showdown at Tsunyi the dominant figure in the Chinese Communist Party. Chu Teh continued as commander-in-chief of the Red Army.

In *Mao Tse-tung in Opposition 1927-1935*, John E. Rue claims, "at least they [that is, the former ruling cliques in the Committee] were willing to give Mao and Chu a chance to try their generalship—perhaps secretly hoping that they too would fail. In retrospect, Tsunyi is the point at which the mass flight of the Red Armies stemmed and the Long March began; when Chu Teh's superb generalship and Mao Tse-tung's political acumen united to turn defeat into victory."

The showdown at Tsunyi had moved Mao Tse-tung to the top spot in the Chinese Communist Party, but it did not solve his immediate problems. The Red Army was still surrounded. It had no place to go, since the plan to take Chungking and unite with the Fourth Front Army in north Szechuan was now impossible. Chu Teh would do the fighting and do it brilliantly, but deciding basic strategy and direction was Mao's job.

Also, in taking his bold stand against the Central Committee, Mao was directly bucking Stalinism. Stalin was a vicious man when crossed. Mao had no way of telling what Stalin would do.

These political problems would have to be settled later. The most pressing problem was to get the Red Army out of its trap. Mao called Chu Teh to a meeting just between the two of them. They met in a back corner of the garden in what had been the home of Governor Wang of Kweichow.

"Where do you want to go?" was all Chu Teh asked.

Mao did not reply in words. He stabbed his finger at a spot on a worn map spread out in front of them. Chu Teh looked at the spot Mao indicated. He nodded and appeared unconcerned, but he must have realized the awesome difficulties that lay between them and that location, which was far to the north in the shadow of the Great Wall of China and close to the border of Inner Mongolia.

What they had gone through up to now had been terrible, but what lay ahead was an even more frightful ordeal.

4

ex

Chu- Mao: The Double Man

The location Mao Tse-tung chose for the Red Army to make its stand against annihilation was at Yenan in Shensi province. It was a remote, impoverished area that could be defended easily—if the Red Army could ever get there.

The distance to Yenan from their location at that time, in Tsunyi, Kweichow, is approximately the same as the distance across the United States from Washington, D.C. to San Francisco, California. The Red Army would have to walk every step of the way. During the first half of the march, they could expect to be hammered night and day by Kuomintang troops bent on their slaughter. Chu Teh estimated the difficulties and told Mao they would be lucky to arrive in Yenan with ten thousand of the original hundred thousand who had left Kiangsi in October, 1934.

He did not expect all these casualties to fall before enemy guns. There would be little opposition from the Nationalist army if they could cross the Tatu River in Szechuan. But when Kuomintang opposition slackened, Nature would take over with a different war. The ice, snow and high-altitude storms in the mountains would be terrible to face. Then, beyond the glacial mountains, they would encounter the weird Grasslands. None of the men had ever seen the Grasslands, but reports painted a dire picture. In that area they would be in a remote section of China rarely penetrated by the Chinese. It was inhabited by aborigine tribes who were sworn to kill any outsider.

The terrific odds against success did not seem to discourage Chu Teh. Several who knew him well said he always seemed to enjoy life best when things were toughest. It was claimed that his good humor in the face of the worst adversity was not a sham to keep up his troops' morale; he really did enjoy trouble.

Even so, Chu Teh could not have gained his tremendous military reputation—acknowledged by leading observers in both East and West—if he had not been eminently practical. No leaders in history have had a better understanding of guerrilla warfare than Mao and Chu Teh. Those two did not strike out blindly across the wildest section of Asia with only a vague hope of success. Mao Tse-tung had been planning that move for weeks and had considered every angle.

Now he and Chu Teh talked long into the night, seeking flaws in Mao's reasoning. They did not fear failure, for their lives as revolutionists had been a series of failures. The important thing was that they were like rubber balls; they bounced back when dropped by misfortune. Often they bounced higher than they were dropped. Failure to both men was but a platform upon which to build and launch a new attack.

One of the major problems that occupied their talks both directly after the Tsunyi conference and in the crucial weeks that followed was how the Red Army could cross the great gorge of the Tatu River farther up in Szechuan. It was here that the Taipings had finally been destroyed during their rebellion seventy years before. Both men were well acquainted with the full history of the Taiping Rebellion. In fact, many of the rules Chu Teh enforced in his army had come directly from the revolutionary ideas of the Taipings.

Both men knew that the last of the Taipings' army had tried to escape the Manchus' fury by making a Long March of their own, and that that march had ended in total disaster at Tatu Gorge in the exact spot their own route would lead them. They also knew how the young Chiang Kai-shek had worshipped the scholar-soldier who had led the Manchu troops to the slaughter of the Taipings at Tatu.

However, Mao did not believe that history ever totally repeated itself, and he said so on several occasions. Now he and Chu analyzed and reanalyzed the Taiping failure so that their own Long March would avoid the mistakes of the Taipings.

But before they could put their revised plans into commission, they had to extricate the Red Army from its dangerous position in Kweichow. Chu Teh argued against immediate retreat. The Red Army was exhausted. Its ranks were one-third depleted. Food and munitions stocks were low. Mao agreed that they should maneuver in Kweichow until they could rebuild their strength.

Actually a disagreement between the two was something no one could ever remember seeing. Since Mao and Chu Teh had first joined together at Chingkanshan mountain the two men had worked as one man. They worked so closely that it became the habit to refer to them as Chu Mao, as if they were one man. The term was so widely used that more than one foreign correspondent referred in his dispatches to "General Chu Mao," leader of the Red Bandits.

As revolutionists, each man complemented the other. Mao, although an able enough military leader, as he had proved to be on occasion, was more deeply involved in basic revolutionary strategy and in the devious politics and organization necessary to stage that revolution successfully. Chu Teh, almost unique among generals of any nation, was a firm believer in the value of political direction of an army. Where other generals huffed and complained at "political interference in purely military matters," Chu Teh sought it. The defeats he suffered as a result of the Central Committee's blunders had not dampened his feelings in this matter. He felt more strongly than ever that the Red Army could not succeed without proper political direction. After the retreat to Chingkanshan he found the perfect political commissar in Mao Tse-tung. The two then gradually were absorbed into the "double man," Chu Mao.

While their thoughts on politics and military matters ran along the same course, in personality the two men were as different as the sun and the moon. They were both tall for Chinese, and thin. Mao's pictures show a generally unsmiling face with a somewhat dreamy look. Chu Teh is invariably shown with a broad smile. Mao generally went bareheaded. His hair was parted in the middle and fell in bushy bangs on each side of his head. Chu Teh always wore the peaked Red Army uniform cap with a red star on the front. Chu Teh was eight years older than Mao, but this did not affect their relationship. Mao, in contrast to his chubby, Buddhalike appearance as an old man, then looked like an underfed peasant poet, which he was. Chu would have been a casting director's choice for a tough old top sergeant with a heart of gold. Both men could show surprising tolerance when dealing with soldiers and peasants but could reverse themselves and display frightening cruelty when dealing with landlords and enemy officials. Above all else, they were dedicated to Communist ideals as they—*not* Moscow—interpreted them.

The two men were as different in background as they were in personality. Mao was born in Hunan province on December 26, 1893. His native village of Shao Shan lay in a valley formed by three mountains. The region was famous in those days for its fine-flavored hogs, its peppercorns, and its excellent-quality rice.

Not very much is known of his childhood. Mao himself gave Edgar Snow a little information. Most of this was about his re- bellion against the strict discipline of his father. Two brothers, Emi Siao and Siao-yu, each wrote a book in which they verified much that Mao told Snow. The brothers, one a Russian-based Communist and the other a Nationalist living in South America, knew Mao in the days of the Red ruler's youth. Emi Siao called his book *Mao Tse-tung, Childhood and Youth*. Nationalist Siao-yu wrote *Mao Tse-tung and I were Beggars*.

The Mao family were farmers but quite well-to-do for their area. The father, Mao Jen-sheng, lost the family farm in his youth and left home to join the army to keep from starving. In time the elder Mao was able to save a little money. Since pay was meager in the Chinese army, he probably made a small stake by looting, a time-honored profession of professional soldiers.

After a time Mao Jen-sheng came back to his native village and increased his stake by judicious trading. Within two years he was able to buy back his lost farm. He married a girl from a village fifteen miles upriver and made a home for his wife, his father, and—eventually—three sons and a daughter. Mao Tse-tung was the first of the sons.

The elder Mao was a born capitalist. From the very first he was an extremely frugal man, and he put all his surplus money into more land. Mao told Edgar Snow that the family consumed only half the rice they grew. The rest his father traded. At first, the elder Mao used the money to buy more land, but later he set up a small rice broker's shop to buy from the other farmers and sell later at a profit.

Mao told Edgar Snow: "After my father became a 'rich' peasant, he devoted most of his time to the rice business. He hired a full-time laborer for the farm and put his children to work on the farm, as well as his wife."

Emi Siao says that Mao began working on the farm when he was six years old, planting rice and acting as a human scarecrow to frighten birds from the ripening grain. At eight he started attending a village school, but that did not lessen his farm work. As soon as Mao learned to use the abacus, his father set him to keeping the rice sales accounts.

The elder Mao was an old-fashioned man who was emperor in his own home. His son was a born rebel who absolutely refused to take the humble, subservient role that tradition assigns to Oriental children. Life between the two was one constant battle. Mao grew up hating his father and the kind of life the old man stood for. When Mao was ten he ran away from home but was brought back. At thirteen, he threatened to commit suicide by jumping into a pond on the farm. His father had upbraided him in front of guests, calling him lazy and stupid.

Mao did not lose all his battles with his stern old father. Siao-yu tells of one such event. After Mao learned to read he devoured the Chinese classics, including *All Men are Brothers* and *The Three Kingdoms*. It was his habit to steal away from his work to a secret place under a pine tree that grew beside an old tomb adjoining the Mao family farm.

One day when Mao was supposed to be carrying manure to fertilize the rice, his father found him reading behind the tomb. Under an agreement they had reached after Mao threatened to drown himself, the old man no longer beat his son. But the elder Mao had not lost his voice. He ranted and raged. Mao protested that he had carried five loads in his yoke buckets. (This is the familiar Chinese coolie way of carrying loads. A yoke fits across the back of the coolie's neck and on his bowed shoulders, permitting him to carry two buckets or loads.) Mao Senior claimed that fifteen loads was a suitable day's work.

He left and returned in the evening to check Mao's work. He found his son reading again in the shadow of the tomb. The old man began to rage again, but Mao pointed out that he had that afternoon carried fifteen loads, which his father had said was a day's labor. This, he claimed, entitled him to return to his reading.

Another family feud erupted when Mao was fourteen. His father, eager to provide himself with grandchildren to carry on the Mao family name and properly care for his ancestors' tombs, provided Mao with a wife. The fourteen-year-old boy rebelled at the idea of being saddled with a wife, especially one six years older than he. He flatly refused to live with the woman or even look at her.

His great ambition was to attend school in the city. Eventually he got his way. The authorities differ on how it came about. Some say that he was permitted to go after convincing his father that an education would enable him to make more money for the family. Siao-yu tells a different tale. He claims that the elder Mao refused to permit the boy to leave because he needed him at home for a harvest hand. Mao found out how much it would cost to hire a laborer, borrowed that amount from a teacher, and gave it to his father.

Evidence indicates that this story may be as much of a fairy tale as Parson Weems' story of George Washington cutting down the cherry tree. There are several records of the elder Mao's threatening to cut off his son's allowance, which indi-

cates that Mao had both his father's permission to go to school
and financial support while he was there.

School at first was unhappy for the country boy. His clothes
were shabby, and he was sneered at by the sons of richer
parents. In time he worked out his social problems and made
friends. His best friend at this time was Emi Siao, and later
Mao became close to Emi's brother, Siao-yu.

The Siao brothers, although sons of well-to-do parents, had
radical leanings, and their interest gradually inclined Mao to
the left. This came naturally to him for he had been a rebel all
his life.

In his early years Mao had been a devout Buddhist, but the
cruelties, famines and deaths he saw made him doubt all reli-
gions. Confucius he rejected simply because the elder Mao
quoted the famous sage. He hated his father and everything
the old man represented. There was a temple to Confucius in
his village, and Mao told friends his boyhood ambition was to
burn it down.

As time passed, he moved on to a larger school in Changsa,
the capital of Hunan. There he met other radicals, and in
1911, when the Chinese Revolution broke out, he joined the
Army.

Army life was miserable for the young recruit. He went
through training and acted as a servant for officers but saw no
fighting. When hostilities ended, with Sun-Yat-Sen agreeing
to back Yuan Shih-kai for the presidency of the new republic,
Mao was mustered out of the service. He then entered the
Teacher's Training School in Changsha along with his friend
Emi Siao. That was in 1912, and he remained there until 1918.

During these six years he read widely, studying socialism
and taking part in radical discussions and groups. But it was
not until 1920, while working as a librarian, that he became
acquainted with Marxism. This record is supported by a

statement Mao made to Edgar Snow: "Three books especially carved my mind. . . . These books were *The Communist Manifesto,* translated by Chen Wang-tao, the first Marxist book ever published in Chinese; *Class Struggle* by Kautsky; and a *History of Socialism,* by Kirkupp. By the summer of 1920 I had become, in theory and to some extent in action, a Marxist, and from that time on I considered myself a Marxist. In the same year I married Yang Kai-hui."

Miss Yang was the quiet, intellectual daughter of a former professor of Mao's. Siao-yu leaves the impression in his book that Mao was the young lady's second choice and that Siao-yu was her unrequited love. She may also have been Mao's second choice, as well. Just before marrying Yang Kai-hui, Mao had founded a cultural bookshop in cooperation with a radical young woman whom all his friends expected him to marry.

What broke them up is not clear. In any event, Mao married Yang Kai-hui. They had two children before she was executed by the Kuomintang in 1927. Her only crime seems to have been that she was the wife of Mao Tse-tung, by then a "Red bandit" with a price on his head.

In 1921 Mao was one of the thirteen men who met secretly at a girl's school in Shanghai to form the Chinese Communist Party. The Comintern had a representative at that meeting, and from the first the Party was Russian-dominated. In the beginning, Mao tried to work with them. For a time he attempted to organize workers in the city as the Party line dictated. Soon, he began to go his own way, rejecting the Stalinist policy of ignoring the peasants. Then he devoted himself exclusively to working in rural areas.

He began organizing guerrilla groups among the peasants, fighting where and how he could for the next seven years. A disastrous defeat caused him to flee to Chingkanshan. There, in the volcanic peaks of the Hunan mountains, he met Chu Teh, beginning the association that led to the creation of "Chu Mao," the double man.

As for Chu Teh, up to the time he joined forces with Mao Tse-tung, he had lived a curious life. In later years when it became popular for Communist leaders to have humble origins, Chu Teh was listed as coming from a peasant family. Before the revisionists got to work on his life, the story had been quite different.

Agnes Smedley in her biography of the great general, *The Great Road,* claims that Chu Teh's family had been poor tenants on the estate of a landlord whose harsh treatment of his tenants earned him the title "Lord of Hell." She paints a dire picture of the family's life under bitter conditions. On the other hand, Edgar Snow, who also knew Chu Teh, traces this report of the general's lowly origin to an inaccurate Comintern biography published in 1936. Snow calls Chu Teh "this scion of a family of landlords" and pictures him as "rising to power and luxury and dissipation while still young."

Chu Teh was born on December 12, 1886. During his youth there were many men still around who remembered the Taiping Rebellion from firsthand knowledge. The boy drank up tales of the fighting, and that had a double influence upon him, guiding him toward a life of soldiering and the life of a revolutionist.

He seems to have received a good education, for he was able in 1906, at the age of 20, to pass the stiff state examinations to qualify for civil service. The next year he was appointed a physical culture instructor but quit in 1908 to enter Yunnan Military Academy to prepare for duty in the Yunnan Provincial Army. Edgar Snow suggests that Chu Teh received the academy appointment through the political influence of his family. This may have been true, but his rapid rise in the army was due solely to outstanding ability.

He graduated as a second lieutenant and fought the Manchus in the Yunnanese army of Warlord Tsai Ao during the Revolution of 1911. By 1912 he was promoted to the rank of major, and later he became a member of Dr. Sun Yat-sen's Kuomintang Party. In another four years, still serving under General Tsai Ao, Chu Teh was a brigadier general known throughout the Republican Army as a fierce fighting man.

He was a special favorite of Tasi Ao, but all his promotions were won by merit. There is a story about how he first came to Tsai Ao's notice. The warlord had just taken over the Yunnan army, and called his officers to report on the condition of their companies.

Chu Teh, then a second lieutenant, stepped forward. He reported that his company commander and two thirds of the troops had deserted. He added that he had pursued them and forced the men to return, but that the commander was still missing.

"We don't need him anymore," Warlord Tsai Ao replied. "You are the new commander."

In 1916 Chu Teh received a great emotional shock when his young wife, his best friend, and his beloved commander, Tsai Ao, all died within a few weeks of each other. He turned to opium for relief from his sorrow. The narcotic addiction that followed, however, did not interfere with his rise in the Yunnan government. He held his position in the Yunnan Provincial Army and concurrently held the position of police commissioner of Yunnanfu (Kunming).

Yunnan then had a proverb claiming that all public officials were thieves and opium addicts. Chu Teh was no exception. Snow reports: "Chu Teh followed the example of his superiors and manipulated the privileges of office to enrich himself. . . . He went in for a harem, too . . . He built them and his progeny a palatial home in the capital of Yunnan."

Snow then claims that Chu Teh's love of reading influenced his subconscious idealism, causing him suddenly to change his ways in 1922. He pensioned off his harem beauties and his wives and went to Shanghai, where he joined a revolutionary group.

The basic facts are as Snow relates, but the immediate cause of Chu Teh's sudden change was something less than idealism. He had suffered some disastrous defeats in battle. In one of these, his two brothers, whom he had persuaded to join the army, were killed. Chu Teh blamed himself for the death of his brothers and blamed his opium smoking for the loss of the battles.

He was also greatly depressed by conditions in China at that time. Sun Yat-sen was fighting to bring the country under his control, but the majority of the provinces were still ruled by warlords who maintained their positions by blood and terror. Conditions were so bad that Chu Teh decided that a Russian-type of Communism was China's only hope. If current conditions continued, the country would be destroyed and then dismembered by greedy foreign nations.

Chu decided to resign from the army and offer his services to the revolutionary group in Shanghai. Friends dissuaded him, however, pleading that they badly needed his fighting ability in Yunnan. He stayed, but his undeniable ability was not sufficient to build a new fighting force out of the opium-sodden troops at his command. Most of the men either had been forced into uniform or had joined to keep from starving. They had no will to fight. It was there that Chu Teh first realized that political indoctrination was essential to building a fighting spirit. That was why he got on so well with his political commissars later. Soldiers need an idea to fight for.

Then Chu Teh was decisively defeated in a battle near Kunming. He and twelve officers barely escaped alive. They fled across the Yangtze and escaped into Tibet, where they lived for a time with a famous bandit chief.

When the search for him died out, Chu Teh went to Shanghai. On the way he crossed the famous swinging bridge over the Tatu River gorge where the Taipings had had their last stand. As he crossed the bridge, Chu Teh recalled the stories he had heard in his youth about the heroic last stand of the Taipings. Perhaps, as a military man himself, he thought of battle strategy and what he would have done had he been in the Taipings' place. As fate would have it, he would—thirteen years later—find himself back in this same spot fleeing with an army from a vengeful enemy just as the Taipings had fled from the Manchus. His situation then would be just as desperate as the Taipings' had been.

Chu had already realized that opium was his downfall—and it may even have been the reason for his military failures at the last. He suddenly gave up the pipe and fought the craving as he made his way to Shanghai. In Shanghai he entered the French Hospital there for additional treatments and then sailed for Europe. A year earlier, he had transferred $10,000 to a Paris bank. However, he went to Germany instead of France because it was the home of Karl Marx. There he contacted the German Communist Party and studied Marxism. Just before leaving Shanghai he had joined the Chinese Communist Party. The man who introduced Chu Teh into German Marxist circles was Chou En-lai, the present premier of Red China.

Chu Teh left Germany after being arrested and detained for a while by the Germany police because of his Marxist associations. He went to Paris for a short time. Then, on the advice of his Communist friends, Chu Teh went to Russia, where he could study Communism in a national setting. He studied for less than a year in the Eastern Toilers' University and then returned to Shanghai. While this political education was something he considered essential to his personal development, he was essentially a man of action rather than a scholar. He missed the battlefield. If ever a man was born to be a soldier, it was Chu Teh.

He was still supporting the Kuomintang at that time, since Sun's party had Stalin's blessing. However, Sun Yat-sen died in 1925, the year Chu Teh returned to China. Chu had no regard for Chiang Kai-shek, who made his bid for power at Sun's death, but he did not break with the Kuomintang party outwardly, although he kept his secret membership in the Communist group.

Kuomintang General Chu Pei-teh, under whom Chu Teh had served before, offered him a general's commission. Chu Teh accepted and was immediately appointed chief of the Bureau of Public Safety in Nanchang, the Kiangsi provincial capital. Chu's new job was to suppress opponents of the Kuomintang government and critics of Chiang Kai-shek.

The usual methods of suppressing political unrest involve terror and firing squads. Chu Teh surprised everyone by maintaining order without excessive bloodshed. Kuomintang officials thought that was owing to fear, for some of Chu's actions as police chief of Yunnanfu had been extremely bloody. This time, however, Chu Teh kept order simply by passing word through secret Communist channels that he wanted no trouble in Kiangsi. The peace thus obtained permitted him to work secretly on plans for a major insurrection against his Kuomintang bosses.

The uprising finally came in 1927. Chu was ordered to suppress it. Instead, he joined Ho Lung, a former bandit chief, to lead the revolt. The insurrection was premature and poorly coordinated among the various Communist groups and guerilla armies. The Communist Party policy of concentrating on the cities and industrial workers had built no support. So when the urban attacks failed, the Red armies fell back to rural areas where the peasants looked upon them as just another bandit gang to be feared and fought. Mao Tse-tung, of all the Communist leaders at the time, was the only one who worked for peasant support.

Chu Teh carefully noted how Mao was protected by the farmers when he retreated, while the rest of the Communists were harrassed and betrayed to the Kuomintang. When Chu's own army collapsed, he gathered his ragged remnants and headed for Chingkanshan, where Mao had taken refuge. From that point on the two men worked together, Mao furnishing the political direction and ideological training for their soldiers, and Chu Teh directing the tactical operations of the army.

The republic—so-called—that they built in Kiangsi showed great promise of enduring, but general Party incompetence caused so many soviets to fail that Chiang was able to bring the full force of his power against Kiangsi, starting Chu Mao, the double man, on the Long March.

Now, at Tsunyi, the leadership passed to Mao. For years he and Chu Teh had argued that the Central Committee's strategy was wrong. They now had to prove their point or perish, along with the entire Communist cause.

5

✄

Blood On The Golden Sands

Tsunyi was the seed from which all future trouble between China and Russia grew. Up to this point the Chinese Communist Party had blindly followed Comintern orders. The election of Mao Tse-tung to the chairmanship of the Central Committee marked the beginning of the break between Chinese and Russian Communism.

The break did not come immediately. The two continued to work together out of necessity, but once Mao was in power it was inevitable that there would be discord between them. Since Mao did not want to lose support of the Stalinists in his party, he felt it necessary to explain his differences. He did this by repeating what he had written in 1930: "Marxist books should be studied, but their study should be coordinated with actual conditions in our country. China is not Russia."

There was little opposition in the Central Committee to Mao's plan to go north to Shensi. There was some consideration given to joining a small soviet operated in northeast Szechuan by Chang Kuo-tao. Mao was very much opposed to that, because Chang was a personal enemy of his and a man with strong personal ambitions of his own. Chu Teh also objected to locating in Chang's soviet, but for a different reason. He argued that the area was too exposed to attack from Nationalist-held Chengtu. If they located with Chang Kuo-tao, it would be only a matter of time until they would be surrounded, as they had been in Kiangsi. In Shensi they would be safe, at least for sufficient time to rebuild their strength.

Now, since their goal was north, they began maneuvering to disguise their true intent. They began by retreating toward the southeast, as if they intended to attack Kunming (Yunnanfu) in Yunnan province. That was excellent strategy, for the Nationalists knew that Chu Teh had been both a general and a police commissioner in Yunnan. He had many friends there and many supporters among the peasants. The Communists could expect plenty of local support.

To counteract this, Chiang sent saboteurs in Red Army uniforms into south Kweichow and northern Yunnan. They burned peasant houses and shot farmers and their families in order to convince the natives that the Reds were bandits. There was little Mao could do to counteract this except to shoot all Nationalist soldiers he caught in Red Army uniforms.

The Communists' pressing need was for new supplies. To this end, Chu Teh headed their columns directly at Kweiyang, the Kweichow provincial capital. The city was strongly defended, but Chu Teh had no intention of wasting his strength on such a formidable target. As the Red Army neared the city, it suddenly split and faded into the hills. Here the troops fell upon company after company of *min tuan*, which were private armies maintained by rich landowners. They were poorly trained, lacking in spirit and quick to surrender.

The Kuomintang troops in Kweiyang, suspecting Chu Teh of a trick to lure them out of their prepared positions, did not immediately follow the Red Army. This gave Chu Teh considerable time to loot government warehouses and provincial stores and to extort money and rice from the wealthy merchants in the smaller towns they captured. A goodly amount of ammunition and guns were taken from the *min tuan*, and a large number of prisoners were taken.

The prisoners were carefully screened by Mao's political commissars for possible recruits. They needed men badly, for they were losing several hundred dead each day in the constant fighting. However, they had to be careful. Lately Chiang Kai-shek had been ordering selected men to surrender in order to infiltrate spies into the Communist ranks.

No prisoners were forced to join the Communists. Chu Teh wanted only soldiers who fought because they believed in the Red Army's ideals. He was careful, however, to treat those he could not or would not accept as soldiers in the kindest manner. They were given a strong Communist indoctrination, shown how democratic the Red Army was in contrast to the autocratic Nationalists, and then released. Often they were given Kuomintang money to get them back to their homes.

In most cases the bewildered prisoners had expected to be shot, as the Reds would have been if captured by the Nationalists. The unexpected kindness made a deep impression on them, as it was intended to do. They went away with a totally different view of the Reds and many became partisan fighters for the Communists, which greatly aided future operations. When Ho Lung was forced into his own Long March a year later and crossed this same route, he received invaluable help from men who remembered Chu Teh's humane treatment when they were his prisoners of war.

Mao's father had been a rice merchant, and his son understood all their tricks. As a result the Red Army was able to uncover many secret stores of grain. Often there was so much that the Red Army could not use it all. Then the rest was distributed—along with proper speeches about Communist regard for the poor—to tenant farmers. Such looting was done under a careful system that brought all returns into the army supply larders or the army treasury. It was a firing-squad offense for any soldier to loot for his own personal gain.

It was now March. The weather was continually bad. Low-bellying clouds dripped rain constantly. On the few days when the clouds broke, Chiang's bombers splattered their ranks with bombs. In one of those attacks, Mao's wife, Ho Tzu-hun, was hit by shrapnel. She had to be carried in a litter until she recovered.

Chu Teh's wife, Kang Ke-ching, was also on the march. An Amazon who would have delighted the heart of a modern women's lib advocate, she was a stocky peasant woman who seemed absolutely tireless. Once she had commanded a company of soldiers, and she was very proud of it. Now her work consisted mainly of organizing mass movements of the non-fighting personnel who accompanied the army and conducting propaganda meetings for the soldiers in the evenings when there was no fighting. During the day she marched with the troops, often carrying a wounded soldier on her back. The way she bounced along on the march was in direct contrast to the progress of Mao Tse-tung, who was suffering from a fever and rode hunched over on a horse, his face flushed and haggard.

Kang once told Nym Wales that she had married Chu Teh in 1929 when she was 17 and he was 43. She seemed to regard him more as a comrade than as a lover.

"I took no care of his food or clothes," she said. "His bodyguards did that. [Actually the "Little Devils"] . . . . Chu Teh does not like women to do housework. He cares nothing for the comforts of his personal life. Mao Tse-tung's wife takes good personal care of him, but she has no other work to do, and he does not spend his time at the front as Chu Teh does."

Tireless, always smiling, obviously enjoying the discomforts, Kang Ke-ching always did more than any other single person. "I did this," she told Nym Wales, "in order to encourage the others, because the wife of the commander-in-chief should always be a model for others to follow."

Other women on the march did not fare so well. There were only thirty-six to begin with, and more than half died on the way. One woman, with only two Little Devils ("*Hsiao Kwei*") struggling to help her in childbirth, was blown to shreds by an exploding bomb. Another slipped and smashed against the rocks while trying to follow her husband up the perpendicular cliff in Hunan. Another was ripped by bullets while trying to supply ammunition to a forward machine gun nest. Some just disappeared in the thick of battle or the confusion of retreat. No one knew what happened to them. Years later Mao Tse-tung spoke with great feeling of the tremendous fortitude of those women who made the Long March.

It was bitter, heartbreaking toil every step of the way. Chiang Kai-shek was moving in for the final kill—or so he thought. Crack Kuomintang troops by the thousands were rushed in for the coming battles. Chiang massed them to block any attempt Chu and Mao might make to smash a hole that would permit them to slip through to join the soviet in north Szechuan.

At that point, a sudden, daring raid by Lo Ping-hui deep into enemy-held territory knocked out an enemy regiment. The spoils included badly needed ammunition and a copy of Chiang Kai-shek's battle plan.

Chu Teh and Mao pored over the captured plans. They worked late at night under a canvas fly that had been rigged between two trees to keep the cold March drizzle off their papers, which were spread over a makeshift table.

The two candles, stuck in bottle necks, had burned down to stubs by the time they had finished. It was almost dawn, and the camp was coming to life in preparation for another bitter, weary day. The noise of the cooks and their "Little Devils," struggling to make fires from the damp wood, drowned out the painful cries and whimpers of the badly wounded which had gone on through the night.

The soldiers slept with sodden blankets pulled around them, too weary to be kept awake by the rain dripping on them and the sounds of the kitchen crews chopping wood. After weeks of constant rain, the kitchen police had developed a technique for building cooking fires. They split the wet logs to get at the dry centers. The centers were then set afire with oiled paper, and the burning dried the outside, which eventually ignited. The wet wood threw up clouds of smoke. This was hard on the kitchen crew, struggling to boil rice, but the rain beat the smoke down so that it did not give away their position to the enemy.

Mao slowly filed the maps back in his office knapsack. His fever was worsening, and he looked half dead. Chu Teh was still Chu Teh. He was never sick.

"We'll have to get out of Kweichow," Mao said.

Chu Teh nodded. Captured documents showed that Chiang was massing an overwhelming superiority of troops for a decisive drive against them. The two leaders considered their position, and decided to retreat southwest into Yunnan. Then they hoped to swing directly north to capture a ferry across the upper Yangtze River, which was called the River of Golden Sands by the Yunnanese.

Chu Teh called his divisional commander, ordering them to inform their troops that the Red Army would attack Kunming, the capital. That was done to insure that Chiang's spies would report the information to the Nationalists. When the news reached Chiang, the Kuomintang leader was jubilant. He rushed to Kunming to take personal command of the expected battle.

Chu Teh had no intention of throwing his crippled army against such a major target. After they entered Yunnan, he sent Lo Ping-hui in a diversionary stab at Kunming. The rest of the Red Army suddenly swung north in an attempt to capture a ford over the Golden Sands River and escape into southern Szechuan.

But Chiang discovered the ruse. He threw so many reinforcements in front of them that Chu Mao did not dare risk a showdown fight. The Red Army retreated. At that moment the Communists had no definite objective. Chu Teh was just trying to keep moving so he could avoid a major battle until conditions favored the Red Army.

In April, Chu Teh sent Lin Piao with about ten thousand men to make another stab at Kunming. His intention was to convince Chiang Kai-shek that the Red Army had abandoned plans to cross the Golden Sands River and now would concentrate in earnest on Kunming. In order to confuse the situation and draw enemy bombers away from Lin's column, Chu Teh ordered Lo Ping-hui to attack Tungchuanfu. Also, a large number of absentee landlords made their home in that city. Their ransom would greatly aid the Reds' treasury.

General Lo, like Chu Teh, was a veteran of the Yunnan Provincial Army. He knew the country well and had many friends there. These old friendships paid off.

As Lo told it later: "We soon had the city under siege. The local *min tuan* commander learned that the troops surrounding the city were mine. I had known him in the old days, and he decided to renew our acquaintance. He sent me a letter."

This "renewal of acquaintence" resulted in the surrender of the city without a fight. While Lo's political commissars arrested landlords and merchants, Lo commandeered the city magistrate's official seal. He then published a city order, authenticated by the stolen seal, ordering all boatmen on the

Golden Sands River to concentrate their craft at a certain spot on the river. The order explained that this measure was necessary to protect the boats from the Red Army. The order was dispatched by partisan runners wearing *min tuan* uniforms.

As soon as he received word that the order had been obeyed, Lo stripped the captive *min tuan* garrison of their uniforms and dressed his own troops in them. He then burned all land records and told the tenant farmers that they now owned their land through the courtesy of the Communist Party.

He then set out for the place where the boats were concentrated, which was below Chou Ping, almost directly north of Kunming. Lo himself cut a decidedly comical figure, but this was in keeping with his *min tuan* disguise. He was a big man, and the largest of the stolen uniforms would not button around his huge stomach. He held his pants up with a piece of rope tied about his middle. After a forty-mile forced march, they arrived at the boats in the night. They were not challenged by the guards. Lo took possession and quickly ferried four companies across the Golden Sands River into Szechuan. They had orders to throw up a perimeter guard to prevent any Szechuan troops from attacking the beachhead until after the bulk of the Red Army got across.

Lo now held the ferry but was unable to get the message to Chu Teh and Lin Piao so they could bring their troops to make the crossing. He kept in touch with headquarters by radio but had only one set. It was out of commission, with burned out tubes. He had no spares, since the Red Army depended upon captured Koumintang materiel.

He immediately dispatched runners to inform both Chu Teh and Lin that he held the ferry. The runners were either killed or captured. They failed to make contact with either commander. However, Chu Teh became suspicious when he could not get in touch with Lo. He knew that the other general had headed for the river. Assuming that Lo was in serious trouble, he sent word to Lin Piao to turn back. The two armies then headed north toward the Golden Sands to aid Lo. Again the Nationalists in Kunming feared a trap, and were cautious about following too closely.

From this point on, the story of the river crossing grows more confused. The stories told by different groups do not agree in any way except that the Red Army did cross the Golden Sands. Robert Payne says that the vanguard of the army found the ferry boats pulled up on the opposite side of the river (the Szechuan bank). Soldiers of the Red Army then posed as tax officers and ordered the guards to bring the boats across to the Yunnan side. Then the boats were captured and used to transport the rest of the army across.

Edgar Snow, in *Red Star Over China*, tells an entirely different story. His version says the vanguard did find all the boats pulled up on the Szechuan side of the river. They then captured a local official and forced him to call across the river (which was about two-thirds of a mile wide at that point), and order the guards to send a boat over to pick him up. The boat was captured, and under cover of the coming night the Red Army used the boat to send over soldiers, who overpowered the guards. They then brought back the captured boats. It took nine days to ferry all the soldiers over the river.

Agnes Smedley gives still another account of the river crossing. Her information presumably came from Chu Teh, but that does not necessarily make it right. A commander-in-chief does not know much about the details of his command. She claims that Lin Piao "reached the ferry crossing at Chou Ping Fort, disarmed the astounded Szechuan garrison, seized nine large boats. . . . The rest of the Red Army followed and crossed in safety."

Hsu Meng-chiu, who compiled an official Red Army history, claimed that the Red Academy Cadet Corps captured a nationalist messenger enroute to order all boats burned. That messenger agreed to guide Chu Teh to the boats. All but one had been removed. This one was used under cover of night to ferry over ten soldiers at a time until there were enough to attack the nearby Szechuan garrison.

Each of these stories leaves the impression that a different group succeeded in being first to grab the boats, thus preparing the way for the rest to follow. There are other discrepancies in the stories. They differ on whether the Kuomintang troops attacked before the Red Army made the crossing and whether or not there was fighting on the Szechuan side after the crossing.

The true story of the crossing is that the conflicting stories are all correct. The First Route Army approached the Golden Sands in three different columns. The various writers who have told about the crossing apparently talked individually to different commanders or soldier groups. Each told what his unit did.

Lo Ping-hui reached the river first and got four companies across. (This account is partially supported by Hsu Mengchiu's statement: "Lo Ping-hui's Ninth Division had been cut off. They had to cross at another place.") Lo then sent messengers to tell the others what he intended to do. Those messengers were apparently captured by the Kuomintang.

Then advance scouts for Lin Piao, whose troops were rushing through a 45-mile forced march to get to the river, spotted Lo Ping-hui's four companies on the opposite side of the Golden Sands. Lo's men were still dressed in their captured *min-tuan* uniforms. The scouts rushed back to report to Lin Piao that a considerable force of enemy troops was on the opposite banks of the river.

Lin then altered his line of march, heading toward Chou Ping Fort, a few miles up river from the place where Lo crossed. Lin found only nine boats. The river was two-thirds of a mile wide and the current was swift, for the water plunged down through high mountain gorges. That is why the river was fordable only at certain points. It required thirty minutes just to make a one-way crossing, making the transfer of an entire army a very slow process. The situation became critical when scouts reported that enemy troops from Kunming were advancing again. The Kuomintang forces were slowed by the poor terrain and moving cautiously for fear of an ambush by Red guerrillas. Even so, they were coming faster than Lin Piao could ferry his men across the river.

By that time Lo had discovered Lin Piao's mistake. He sent runners across the river to let Lin know that the troops he saw on the opposite bank were not *min tuan*, despite their uniforms. Lin then sent part of his division upriver to use Lo's boats. That enabled them all to get across the Golden Sands before the Kuomintang's Nationalist Army arrived.

Lin and Chu Teh recombined their forces and started north, leaving Lo at the river to delay the Nationalists' crossing. Lo burned all the boats after paying the owners five thousand Kuomintang dollars for them. This was done to insure their friendship, if the Red Army had to retreat into that area again.

Up ahead, the main mass of the Red Army marched north toward the great mountains as political workers led them in revolutionary songs. Back at the river, Lo Ping-hui was too busy to sing. His troops were spilling their blood and Kuomintang blood on the banks of the Golden Sands. The Nationalists had succeeded in getting some troops across the river. Here they joined with some Szechuan Provincial regiments to smash Lo Ping-hui's defense line.

The battle raged through the night. Lo was unable to use his favorite hit-and-run tactics, for his objective was to stop the enemy advance until the main body of the Red Army could get away. He had no choice but to stand and slug it out. The carnage was frightful on both sides. Half of Lo's forces were slaughtered, and the Kuomintang losses were even greater. At dawn the Nationalists pulled back. Lo regrouped and began a hasty retreat, following the route broken through the hills by the First Front Army.

The enemy were unable to follow immediately, but Kuomintang bombers took up the fight. Their harrassment continued until the Red Army fought their way into the mountains where the planes could not find them.

Here the troops were able to make camps, getting their first rest in days. The first day they did nothing but sleep, but on the second day Chu Teh had them busy with the normal details of military camp life. Rifles had to be cleaned; filthy, bloody clothes washed; festering sores and wounds cleansed with hot water (all medical supplies had long since been exhausted); and the new dead were buried. Hot soups and rice tasted like a banquet after the long days with either nothing or cold rice balls for food.

Chu Teh also insisted on every man's washing his feet each night. It was said that early in his military career, Chu had lost a battle because his men's feet were so sore that they could not walk fast enough. After that, he considered shoes and foot care (to avoid the common soldier's trouble called "trench foot") as important as rifles.

In the evenings the political corps was busy, organizing sing-songs and putting on dramatic plays depicting revolutionary themes. Some of the plays showed the cruelty of Chiang's government; others were romantic, Communist-style. One told about a beautiful girl who entreated her lover to fight with the Red Army and to return to her when "the running dogs of imperialism had been driven from China. The term "running dog" is equivalent to calling someone an SOB in English.

Many of the revolutionary songs were set to Western tunes. Many employed the melodies popular with college glee clubs, familiar drinking songs, and more than one reporter has told of hearing revolutionary songs loudly sung in Chinese to the tune of "Dixie."

Mao and Chu Teh both placed great emphasis on singing and often joined in the sing-songs themselves. While neither sang well, they both sang enthusiastically. New recruits were taught revolutionary songs along with rifle drill. Lo Ping-hui was the only commander on the Long March who did not keep his soldiers singing. He said later, "The main Red Column sang all the time. My men, however, were too busy and tired for singing, being constantly on maneuver." This was because their rear-guard position was more exposed.

Whenever Lo's men had a moment's break, they washed their feet. Chu Teh might forgive them for not singing, but he was totally unforgiving of anyone who failed to keep his feet clean. After that, they ate and then dropped in their tracks to sleep. They were, as Lo Ping-hui once described himself, always sleepy. Sometimes they slept a few minutes, sometimes, if lucky, a few hours, but never all night.

After the sing-songs in the main column, the political corps made speeches. All had a revolutionary slant. Often Chu Teh or Mao would speak. Mao's favorite topic was Japanese aggression against China, which began in 1932 in Manchuria. Mao liked to remind his audience that the "little dwarfs" were tearing away hunks of the Chinese dragon while Chiang Kai-shek's Kuomintang government wasted the country's military resources in fighting their fellow Chinese (that is, the Communists) instead of the foreign enemy.

Often during those rest periods in the evenings members of the political corps put on skits, lampooning the Nationalist government. Former Kuomintang soldiers—often prisoners of war who had enlisted in the Red Army—came forward to tell horrifying stories of service under Chiag Kai-shek. They would be followed by political corpsmen who would then contrast such treatment with the way the Red Army treated its soldiers. In the Red Army, they pointed out, no officer was permitted to curse or strike a soldier. There were no special privileges. Everyone shared alike, eating the same food, wearing the same cheap cloth uniforms, and taking the good and the bad together.

This equality was observed in Mao and Chu's First Front Army and in Ho Lung's Second Front Army, but not in Chang Kuo-tao's Fourth Front Army in upper Szechuan. Chang ruled like a warlord. This attitude, and Chang's special privileges for his friends and officers, would bring him and Mao Tse-tung into conflict later in the Long March.

Every action was designed to build up the morale of the individual soldier, to make him feel an important part of a great movement, and to increase his hatred of the enemy. Kuomintang and landlord atrocities and oppressions of the peasant class were constantly put before the troops, while the Red Army was pictured as the sole champion of the farmers and the coolies.

The festive air of those evening stops could not disguise the tragedy that constantly hung over the march. The entire army hospital had only three doctors. They were assisted by a few women and a group of Little Devils, all under fifteen, who acted as nurses as best they could. The sick and wounded made an unending line. Hundreds died every day, many of whom could have been saved if there had been sufficient doctors and medical supplies.

As general supplies were exhausted or destroyed by enemy bombing, many of the porters turned to carrying the wounded, but most had to hobble along as best they could. Those unable to keep up were given their guns and some money and told to drop out and join partisan groups.

The First Front Red Army had been marching for six-and-a-half months by the time it made the Golden Sands crossing. Chou En-lai, in the course of a 1936 interview, said that Red Army losses up to that time were 45,000, nearly half of the number who had started from Kiangsi at the beginning of the Long March in the October of 1934.

Devastating as those losses were, more were ahead of them as the Red Army approached the Tatu River gorge country, the freezing heights of the Great Snow Mountain, and finally the terrors of the Grasslands. In the next five-and-a-half months they would lose another 48,000 men—more than they had lost in the previous six months.

Edgar Snow, in *Random Notes on Red China*, quotes Chou En-Lai as saying that losses due to actual fighting were less than those from fatigue, sickness, starvation and attacks from tribesmen. The aborigines were fierce fighters. There had been little trouble with the Miao tribesmen in southern Hunan, but now, as the Red's First Front Army crossed the Golden Sands, they headed directly toward a confrontation with the savage Lolos—aborigine tribesmen who had never been conquered and who hated the Chinese with a fierce passion.

Chu Mao—the double leader—well knew the risk of trying to cross the land of the savage Lolos, but they had no alternative. To swing to the right around Lololand would head the badly depleted Red Army straight into Chiang Kai-shek's troops at Chengtu. If they swung to the left to circle Lololand on the outside, they would be forced into the high plateaus of Tibet where they would be at the mercy of equally fierce tribesmen and an extremely hostile environment.

But despite the formidable difficulties that lay ahead, the soldiers fell quickly into line when the bugles blew "Fall in!" The vanguard moved out ahead. The rear guard fell back to guard against an attack from behind. The main columns formed. Those with burdens shouldered their yokes. The Long March resumed. Mao Tse-tung, still ill with fever, was hunched in his saddle. Chu Teh gave his horse to a wounded soldier and walked with his headquarters staff. The doctors, who had worked all night, rode in sedan chairs carried by four soldiers each and tried to sleep in preparation for another grueling night when the column stopped again.

Fatigue had cut deep lines in all their faces. Only Chu Teh and his amazon wife seemed unaffected by the grueling ordeal. The Little Devils, with the ability of the young to recover, were full of energy at the start, although they would tire as the day dragged on.

6

Where the Taipings Died

The Yangtze River rises in the highlands of Chinghai. It draws water from thousands of tributary streams, increasing in size as it rushes through steep gorges between Tibet and Szechuan. Then it cuts into Yunnan as if headed for Thailand, but once inside Yunnan, the great river turns first east and then north and back south again to make a great bend before turning to pass Chungking, the triple cities of Wuhan and Nanking before reaching the sea at Shanghai.

The great bend area encloses the wildest sections of Szechuan. It is the home of the *I-min*, whom the Chinese call the Lolos. At the time of the Great March Lololand was included in Sikang Province and considered a part of Tibet. Sikang no longer shows on Chinese maps. The area, including the Tatu River gorge, is now shown as a part of Szechuan.

The people Westerners call Chinese—those who call themselves Hans—did not originate in China but immi-

grated from the west. When they first came to China, in pre-
historic times, they found the land populated with a variety of
aborigine tribes. These tribes were mongoloid, caucasoid and
negrito. In time some of these aborigines fled south to become
the Negritos of the Philippines, and the Thais, Burmese, Indo-
nesians and Malaysians. The Lolos were one of the aborigine
tribes the Hans were unable to displace. The wild mountain
area where they lived and their exceptionally savage fighting
ability preserved them from Chinese onslaughts right down to
modern times. Lololand covers some 11,000 square miles, and
the Red Army's route led directly through it.

Chu Teh moved his forces toward Lololand in night
marches only. Kuomintang aircraft constantly patroled the
daytime skies, seeking both information on their route and
targets to bomb. The Red Army left the roads at dawn,
dispersing among the trees on the mountain slopes until night
hid them again.

Their goal was now the Tatu River ferry, in the area just
above where the Taipings had met disaster seventy-two years
earlier. It was impossible to disguise their objective now, for
there was no other place they could go. Chiang, also an avid
student of the Taiping Rebellion, moved his headquarters to
Chengtu, east of the Tatu River, and began plans to repeat the
Taiping massacre with the Communists as the victims this
time.

The distance from the Golden Sands River crossing to the
Tatu ferry crossing was about 120 miles. The first twenty
miles before they entered Lololand were in Chinese territory.
All the *min tuan* soldiers had been pulled out of the local
towns to supplement the Kuomintang Nationalist armies. The
towns the Red Army passed through were undefended.

At Mien Ning the Reds found that the local officials and
merchants had feared them more than the Lolos. They had all

fled into Lololand. There they were captured by the aborigines, stripped of everything but their pants and driven back to face the Red Army.

In the next town, the Reds and the Lolos fought their first battle. The Chinese had deserted the city at the approach of the Red Army. When Chu Teh sent a group into the town in search of food, they found themselves suddenly attacked by Lolos, who also were intending to plunder the place. Several soldiers were killed on both sides before the Lolos retreated.

After this hasty battle, Mao and Chu Teh held a council of war. Their ability thus far to keep ahead of the Nationalists had been based partly on keeping the good will of local peasants and natives. They had expected to do the same with the Lolo tribes. The unexpected fight had indicated that they would have difficulty in making friends with the aborigines there.

Chu Teh pointed out that the Red Army could not possibly fight its way completely across Lololand and arrive at the Tatu ferry in any shape to beat off the troops that Chiang Kai-shek was sure to rush in to block their crossing. Mao agreed. He and Chu Teh had a unique way of always seeing things in the same light. Chu Teh then pointed out that making friends was a political matter. He handled the fighting end; it was Mao's job to handle political contacts.

Again Mao agreed, but he offered no immediate suggestion as to what they could do. Earlier, he had sent emissaries with messages telling the Lolo chiefs that the Red Army had peaceful intentions. Mao's messengers had been slaughtered and the peace overtures ignored. Mao was handicapped, because very few Chinese had ever had any contact with the Lolos, and nobody understood them or their customs. Then Lin Piao brought a corps commander named Liu Pei-cheng to see Mao. Liu had been a former *min tuan* officer in Szechuan.

He had fought the Lolos for years and could speak their language.

What Liu told Mao was not encouraging. The Lolos had a vicious hatred for all things Chinese, and they jealously guarded their independence.

The Lolo tribes were of indeterminate origin. In some features they resemble the Tibetans. However, blue and hazel eyes are not uncommon among them, which indicates that they are probably a mixture of Mongolian and Caucasian types.

The Lolos, Liu told Mao, lived a simple life. They hunted mountain animals, raised sheep and cattle, and practiced a primitive form of "slash and burn" agriculture. They did not employ fertilizer but cleared a forest track by cutting and burning the timber, farming until the soil was exhausted, and then migrating to a new location. They dressed in long trousers with a blanket top somewhat resembling the dress of certain Andean tribes of South America.

Politically, the Lolos were divided into numerous small tribes, each ruled by its own chief. The tribes did not work together unless facing an invader. The people themselves were divided into the "Black" Lolos and the "White" Lolos. Apparently this designation originated as "Black Leg" and "White Leg" and referred to their manner of dress. The Black Lolos were the dominant group and made slaves of both the White Lolos and the Chinese they captured in the continuing war with Szechuan.

When Liu spoke of the Black and White Lolos, Mao, still suffering from fever, straightened a little from his slumped position and nodded slightly to Chu Teh, who nodded back. Communist divide-and-conquer-tactics are at their best when two forces are arrayed against each other.

However, it appeared that there was nothing they could do about securing freedom of passage through all Lololand. They would have to make a deal with a tribal chief, but as soon as they passed his mountain or valley, they would face a new and hostile tribe that must be placated before the Red Army could go on.

It now appeared impossible for the Red Army to fight its way across Lololand. Widely ranging Lolo bands, knowing the wild, densely timbered terrain, could cut the invaders to pieces. They were as experienced guerrilla fighters as the Communists.

While Mao was questioning Liu, runners brought word that an engineering company that had been sent ahead to construct bamboo bridges over streams had been cut off and destroyed when they entered Lololand.

Shortly after this, a company on the Red Army's right flank captured a small town where several Lolo tribesmen were held captive. They were taken directly to Mao, who talked to them through Liu's interpretation.

The captives expected execution, but instead they were warmly welcomed. Mao explained to them that just as there were Black Lolos and White Lolos who were enemies, there were Red Chinese and White Chinese who fought each other as well. He explained that the soldiers who had fought the Lolos in the past had been White Chinese.

"We both have the same enemy, the White Chinese," Mao argued. "Why can't we work together against our common enemy?"

One of the Lolos was a chief who had been marked for execution by the Nationalists. He gave Mao a sly look.

"How can we fight with you when we have no guns?" he asked.

Mao did not hesitate. He turned to a Little Devil orderly and ordered guns brought for all the Lolo captives. He then invited them to see how the Red Army lived and trained, adding that they were welcome to go home or stay and fight the common enemy with the Reds. They were shown a group of recruits drilling. These had been picked up from *Min tuan* deserters to fill the depleted ranks. None of these recruits, badly needed as replacements were, would be allowed in battle until they had undergone an extensive political education.

The Lolos were permitted to listen as shrewd political examiners tested each recruit to be sure that he was properly indocrinated with Communist ideals and not just pretending. These sessions usually began by questioning the recruits in a group. The political examiner would ask:

"How many rich men and rich men's sons are in the Kuomintang army?"

The recruits would answer truthfully that they saw none in the government service.

The next question was: "How many Kuomintang officers ate the same food as you did when you were in their army?"

The answer, of course, was that no Kuomintang officer had ever eaten with them while they served with the Nationalists.

Since so many of the Nationalists' conscriptees were from farming areas, the next questions generally turned to Kuomintang treatment of farmers, and ended by pointing out how the Red Army respected the peasants' property, and how everything received from farmers was paid for in good money.

Then recruits were encouraged to get up and tell about any harsh treatment they received in Chiang's army. They were followed by a political commissar who reminded them that no officer was permitted to strike or curse a man in Chu Teh's command.

These rap sessions were followed by the usual song, and if time and the enemy permitted, another little play, put on by actors in the political corps.

The Lolos were greatly impressed by the apparent comradeship in the Red Army. There was not time to give them the regular indoctrination that Red Army recruits get. Their instruction period was compressed from several weeks into two days. Even so, several of the aborigines asked to be permitted to go along with the Red Army. Mao agreed with delight. They could be very useful later in dealing with their fellow Lolos as the Red Army went deeper into Lololand.

The Lolos who wanted to return to their tribe were given their guns. There was a risk that those presents might be turned against the Red Army later, but Mao felt that such a gift would be the most dramatic kind of assurance that the Reds trusted the Lolos and genuinely wanted friendship.

Although it was extremely dangerous, Liu volunteered to accompany the freed Lolos back to their home. While the gratitude of the captives seemed sincere, he had no way of knowing how other Lolos might feel about a visit from a member of their traditional enemy.

Fortunately, the Lolo chief was impressed by the stories of the returning captives. He listened carefully as Liu repeated Mao's story of the two kinds of Chinese, comparing them to the two kinds of Lolos. He swore a blood-brother oath with Liu, climaxed by each man's drinking chicken blood to signify that if either broke the oath he would be as craven-hearted as the chicken.

The ceremony assured the Red Army safe passage only through that chief's valley. When the Red Army climbed the next mountain, it was in another tribe's territory. Those new tribes owed the Communists no gratitude for saving any of their members. So new negotiations had to be carried on.

In this matter Mao was aided not only by the Lolos who had joined the Red Army but also by guides furnished by the chief who had become Liu's blood brother. The Lolo mediators did manage to prevent war, but the other tribal chiefs drove shrewd bargains before they would permit the Reds to cross their land.

Hsu Meng-chui told Nym Wales: "These Lolos were first-class confiscators. We were not too much amused to find someone who could do this better than ourselves. . . . The

tribesmen were never satisfied and took more and more from
us. They looked in our pockets. . . In fact, they stole
everything portable that the Red Army had to spare."

Only the iron discipline of the Red Army prevented angry
Red soldiers from shooting the predatory tribesmen. Mao had
given the strictest orders that all friction must be avoided.
Despite all the indoctrination talk of democracy in the army,
punishment for infraction of rules was swift and sure—
including, if the offense warranted, the firing squad.

During this time—and despite his fever—Mao worked
closely with Liu and the Lolos in order to learn and respect all
Lolo taboos and customs. An increasing number of tribesmen
asked to join the Reds. Chu Teh replied: "Any one who hates
the Nationalists as they do and can fight the way they do is my
kind of a man." He welcomed them into the ranks of the Red
Army, gave them recruit drill, and then sent them to political
school. Some became so proficient at Marxism that they were
later sent back to Lololand to teach their fellow tribesmen.

The Red Army spent three weeks in Lololand, emerging
thankfully at the end of May, 1935. During that time the thick
timber cover in the aborigine territory had effectively shielded
them from Chiang Kai-shek's observation planes.

It was a complete surprise to the Kuomintang when the Red
Army suddenly burst from the shelter of Lololand. Chiang
Kai-shek in Chengtu was still trying to assemble sufficient
troops to cut Mao and Chu Teh off at Tatu gorge. The
Szechuan provincial troops in the area were completely
unprepared to do battle. None had expected the Red Army to
get through Lololand so quickly and easily. Some of Chiang's
generals had even argued that Mao would never get past the
Lolos at all. Speaking from their own experience with the
fierce aborigines, they felt that the Red Army would be cut to
pieces.

At the edge of the Lolo forests, the vanguard, led by the
First Division of the First Army Corps, surprised a force of

several hundred Szechuan provincials. There was no fight; the Szechuanese surrendered. Chu Teh seized their rice. However, although the Red Army larders were sadly depleted, Mao Tse-tung made sure that his troops took only what they badly needed. The rest was distributed to poor tenant farmers as part of Mao's long-standing policy of demonstrating the Red Army's concern for the poor.

For the same reason, several of the higher-ranking officers captured in the Szechuan group were put on public trial for atrocities they had committed against the peasants. The farmers came forth to curse and testify against the accused. Then the guilty men were convicted and turned over to the peasants for execution.

Such actions slowed down the march, and there really was not time for that. However, Mao believed that the psychological value was worth the short delay. Chiang Kai-shek, in his Kuomintang propaganda, was continually talking of agrarian reform and doing nothing. Mao Tse-tung knew that he could not establish the Communists as the true champions of the people if he only talked reform as Chiang did.

On each stop, no matter how short, the political corps tried to get peasants together for a mass meeting. Even though his fever was getting worse, Mao talked at as many mass meetings as he could. While the other speakers reminded the peasants of the cruel treatment they had received at the hands of their landlords and the Kuomintang Army, Mao talked on a more lofty plane. He traced the history of the Communist movement in China. He likened it to a candle's small flame but reminded his audience that even the tiniest spark of fire could—and in this case would—turn into a mighty holocaust that would sweep everything before it.

Mao was not a great speaker, or even a dynamic one, but he had a sincerity and clarity that went straight to the hearts of his audiences. Chu Teh was a good speaker but rarely spoke at those mass meeting of peasants. Whenever he could get a chance, however, he spoke to groups of soldiers. He had them sit in a circle around him, and he turned first one way and then the other so that all could see his face. When he talked to soldier groups he never failed to remove his peaked gray-blue cap with the little red star in the center. He did not replace the cap until he had finished talking.

Chu Teh liked to remind the troops of the sacrifices of freedom fighters of the past. He was especially fond of talking about the Taipings. He presented the stories in such a way that his soldiers felt that they were carrying on the tradition of those heroes of yesterday.

The peasant troops were very much impressed. Most of them had been tenant farmers, given no more consideration than dirt in the streets by their landlords and their warlord rulers. Now, for the first time in their lives, someone was making them feel important and giving them a mission in life beside grubbing from day to day to eke out a bare existence.

They had, as soldiers, say, "found a home" in the Red Army. No matter how difficult their lives were in the Long March, most of them found the conditions preferable to what they had known before. They were willing to follow wherever Chu Mao led, with blind faith in their two leaders.

During the brief halt of the central column, a vanguard division under Lin Piao had pushed on to the banks of the Tatu River. They rushed the town of Anshunchang, which had grown up around the river ferry in one of the few places where the turbulent river could be crossed.

The Tatu is a short river, feeding out of the rugged mountains in western Szechuan and tumbling down through fantastically steep gorges and defiles in a due south course that suddenly swings to the east and a final junction with the Yangtze. Its entire length is not over 400 miles. Its watershed is tremendous, so that at all seasons it plunges and roars in an eternal flood stage through the steep defiles. The noise of the river is so great that it can be heard miles away.

Spies reported back to Lin Piao that there were Szechuan troops on the opposite banks of the river, but that their commander and a small guard force were on the Anshunchang side. The commander had crossed the river in one of the three ferries to visit relatives in Anshunchang. This ferry was still tied to the south dock. The other two ferries were on the north bank.

Lin Piao did not hesitate. He struck Anshunchang at dawn, easily overcoming the hundred-man guard, but the commander escaped. Then the Red Army rushed on to capture the ferry. Several crewmen were killed in the fighting, and the rest of the ferry crew fled. This put Lin Piao in a difficult position. Because of the darkness and the tremendous roar of the river, the Szechuan troops on the opposite bank were not yet aware that the Red Army had taken Anshunchang. There was still time to surprise them, but there was no one to run the ferry, which could carry eighty men.

Lin Piao, and Chu Teh also, had ridden this ferry years before. Lin knew that the river was so swift and the rocks so treacherous that none but natives who knew the river well could row the big ferry across the torrent. At least seventeen boatmen were needed. Soldiers fanned out to seek them while Lin called Chu Teh over the radio. Then he waited in an agony of suspense for his men to find boatmen who knew the river.

The main body of the army started to move to join Lin Piao. Hastily, the political workers distributed guns to peasants they felt would make good partisan fighters, shouted a few last revolutionary slogans, and rushed to join the departing army.

In the meantime, Lin's men did find enough boatmen to man the ferry, but the delay ruined their chance to surprise the enemy on the north bank. They mounted machine guns in the bow of the ferry and pushed off anyway.

The river current was so strong that no boat could cross the river directly. It had to start two miles upstream from its landing point and work itself across. There were eighty-five soldiers aboard, the regular eighty passenger positions, plus five extra who were used at the oars to supplement the undermanned crew.

The heavy boat swung sharply in the current. The crouching men were drenched by spray. The oarsmen strained at their paddles, slowly working the ferry toward the opposite shore. The machine guns were protected from the spray by oiled paper covers. These were jerked off as the boat finally swung in toward the north shore dock, after fighting the roaring river for two hours.

The Red machine gunners sprayed the dock area with a hail of lead to drive the Szechuan defenders under cover. Then, as the ferry bumped the dock, the machine guns paused to give the Red foot soldiers a clear space to charge ahead. When they had found cover, the machine guns began chattering again.

The defenders fell back in confusion. The Reds advanced. Two squads broke away from the main force. They circled to the right and left in an attempt to flank the enemy. One squad got around and climbed the cliff that was directly behind the ferry position. The cliff was part of the pass leading to Chengu.

Realizing what was happening, the Szechuan commander lost his head and ordered men to cut off the advancing Reds. In his frenzy the Szechuanese failed to realize that he was sending his men into the open, where they would be cut down by Red Army machine guns from the ferry. After this, the fight dragged on for several hours, but the Red Army victory was assured by the enemy commander's mistake.

That ferry, along with the other two tied up on the north shore, was sent back for more passengers. The original two-hour one-way trip was lengthened to four hours as the river, fed by heavy rains upstream, became increasingly turbulent. The troop transport was so slow that the rest of the First Front Army arrived and had to bivouac. After four days of ferrying, night and day, the boatmen had succeeded in carrying only the majority of Lin Piao's advance guard.

The delay was frustrating and might mean trouble later on, since it could permit Chiang Kai-sheks troops in Cheng-tu to move west to intercept their route away from the Tatu. However, that was in the future—something to worry about when the time came.

In the meantime the political corps began organizing mass meeting of the people of Anschunchang. The soldiers cleaned their guns and washed their clothing—and feet—in the river. New recruits drilled and listened to hours of political lessons. Mao Tse-tung, his face still flushed with the fever that refused to break, pored over maps and papers from his compartmented knapsack. The supply corps foraged for food, and the tailors—who had carried sewing machines on their backs all the way from Kiangsi—stitched uniforms for the recruits.

Chu Teh set great store by uniforms. He felt that a man could not feel like a soldier until he had one. Once, Chu Teh told Agnes Smedley how happy they had all been when they got their first Red Army uniforms in 1927. It had made all the difference in the world in their morale. "I suppose they would seem very poor beside the uniforms of other nations, but we were very proud," he said.

After that, he always saw that his soldiers had their own uniforms, and he alone was responsible for insisting on carrying sewing machines through every step of the Long March.

Suddenly, on the afternoon of the fourth day, there was an explosion in the middle of the river so loud that it momentarily drowned out the roar of the stream. A geyser of water shot up near the bow of the first ferry, which was in the middle of the river.

The startled army looked up to see a Kuomintang bomber flashing away. Then they ran for cover as another came in down the gorge, flying low to release a stick of bombs. The ferry was hidden by the water thrown up by the explosions.

When the water cleared, they saw that the stern of the ferry was sagging. Half of the eighty passengers were in the water. The uncontrolled boat veered in the swift current and struck another ferry. The collision did not hurt the second boat, but another stick of bombs blew it out of the water. The third—and last—of the ferries was caught at the dock.

By this time, Red machine gunners were shooting at the dive bombers, but none were struck. All the passengers on the heavily loaded boats were swept to their deaths. The river was too swift and turbulent for anyone to go their aid.

Grim commanders hurried to a conference with Mao and Chu Teh. This village of Anschunchang was the exact spot where the Taiping Army had perished while trying to do exactly the same thing the Red Army was now attempting—to make a Long March to escape a vengeful government that was its enemy.

It was a favorite expression of both Mao and Chu Teh that history never repeats itself. They liked to quote Karl Marx's remark that when history tries to repeat itself, the result is always a farce.

Now it appeared that history actually might repeat itself. Chiang Kai-shek—also a student of the Taiping movement—sent a message to his commanders ordering them to repeat the massacre of seventy-two years before.

7

Iron Rings and Blood

Mao and Chu did not appear to be greatly disturbed by what anyone could see was a calamity. Chu Teh always smiled, in good times and bad, so it was impossible to tell if he was ever disturbed. Mao had seen so much trouble, had faced so many defeats, and had run for his life so often that defeats had become a way for life for him.

He did not waste the time he spent each evening mulling over his maps and papers. Mao Tse-tung had a far more brilliant mind than his enemies gave him credit for. His success—and the fact that he kept alive after Chiang put a $250,000 price on his head—can be attributed to his ability to analyze every situation clearly and to plan for both success and failure.

Down through the years it had been Mao Tse-tung who grasped the reins from other faltering hands when things got really tough and who found a way out of their troubles. He had done this in Hunan, in Kiangsi, and again at Tsunyi, when it appeared that the Long March was headed for failure.

Now, with the Red Army facing the fate of the Taipings, Mao did not hesitate or seek unnecessary counsel. He put his finger on a map of Szechuan and said, "There is a bridge here. We will cross it."

The bridge Mao referred to was about a hundred miles up-river, at a village called Lutingchiao. The region was even wilder than that around Anschunchang. The bridge itself was made of huge chains anchored in concrete stanchions that were set on each side of sheer cliffs. The river between them spashed and foamed far below as it struggled to break through the confining gorge walls.

The road to Lutingchiao was narrow, climbing steep moun-tains, winding through narrow defiles, and often shrinking to dangerous ledges hacked in the cliffs over the raging torrent of the Tatu River. For at least half of the hundred-mile march the Red Army could expect to be restricted to single-file marching. It would be slow and dangerous, even if the Kuomintang Army did not catch up in time to force Chu Teh to fight along the way.

However, Chu Mao—the double leader—had no choice. The Red Army was in a trap. They could not cross the Tatu here at Anschunchang without strong boats. There was no place they could get more ferries. The water was too turbulent to use rafts, which they could have made by felling trees. They could not retreat. The mass of Kuomintang troops be-hind them was too great for any chance of victory.

The dangerous road to Lutingchiao and the bridge across the Tatu were no more than a crack in the trap that the Red Army found itself in at Anschunchang. But as Mao Tse-tung pointed out at the commanders' meeting, they had escaped through smaller cracks before. However, in past crises they had several alternatives they could have taken. If one failed, they could turn a different way. This had happened in

Kweichow. When the push on Chungking failed, they fell back, striking at Tsunyi a second time, and then reversed to make a diversionary attack toward Kunming before wheeling for their final charge at the Golden Sands crossing.

Such diversions confused the enemy. Chiang's field commanders never knew which way Chu Mao would strike next. This left them always on the defensive. Now the Red Army was hemmed in. There was only one possible way it could go. Chiang's commanders would be able to plot the Red Army's intentions for the next several days as surely as if Chu Teh had called them in for a planner's briefing.

Still worse, Lutingchiao was the last possible place to cross the Tatu. If they found the bridge destroyed, or if the Kuomintang succeeded in blocking their way, there was no place else to cross. They would then be faced with two alternatives. They could try to fight their way back, which would be sheer suicide, or try to work their way on into Tibet, where they would be at the mercy of vengeful tribesmen who hated all things Chinese.

In his announcement to the commanders, Mao did not dwell on the alternatives. He merely said, as if it were an afterthought, "And should we find the bridge destroyed, then we will find another way—*as we always have!*"

The radios were still working, and Lin Piao, across the river, was notified of the new plans. He immediately began marching along the north shore road toward Lutingchiao. Lin's reputation as a tactician was second only to that of Chu Teh. (Later, Lin Piao became minister of defense for all China.) Lin did not need detailed instructions. He knew that his job was to get to the bridge as quickly as possible and secure the north end, beating back any Kuomintang attempts to bring in new troops from Chengtu.

The road to Lutingchiao was as hard as the early passage they had made over the Nanling Mountains between Kiangsi, Hunan and Kwantung. But then the First Front Army had been fresh. Now its strength had been sapped by the four thousand miles its people had marched in the seven-and-a-half months since they left the Kiangsi soviet in October, 1934.

During those bitter months, at least half of the original marchers had died. The rest had fought nearly every day in some kind of battle, marched and slept in the rain, sweltered under subtropic heat and humidity, and shivered in the cold of the mountain passes. They had eaten well when the Red Army was able to capture food from landlords or could buy rice from peasants. In between, they had gone hungry.

Now they were ragged and dirty and riddled with disease. Many suffered from festering sores caused by poorly treated wounds. Most of those in the troops were young, strong peasant types. But there is a limit to human endurance. It appeared that the Red Army was approaching that limit as it snaked its way over the dangerous mountain road to Lutingchiao.

Mao Tse-tung's fever still refused to break. Lo Ping-hui was scarcely able to stay on his mule. He was suffering so badly from dysentery that he had been forced to give over command of the rear guard troops to Ho Chung-kung. Soldiers at first carried Lo on a stretcher, but his weight required four men. He decided that this was a waste of manpower. He had himself boosted on his mule and rode on as best he could.

Much of the excess equipment the army had brought from Kiangsi had long since been abandoned. Their rice hampers were empty and the ammunition stocks depleted. The men no longer marched. They shuffled along with their heads down, their shoulders drooping under the weight of their packs, and their feet dragging. Even the usually irrepressible Little Devils were subdued as they struggled to keep up with the main column. Only Chu Teh was still Chu Teh. Those who were along during these grueling days all say that their commander never lost his smile or his good humor. Chu Teh was fifty years old. Yet he never rode when things were tough. He continued to give his horse to some wounded man. He walked with the troops and ended the day fresher than any of them, despite the twenty-five years' difference in his age and most of theirs.

Chu's amazon wife, Kang Ke-ching, was equally tireless. It was her opinion that the wife of the commander-in-chief should set an example to the others and she did. Once her remark was repeated to Chu Teh. He smiled wryly and said, "And an example to the commander as well!"

The Red Army was strung out in a long thin line as it struggled over the hills and down into the valleys. Its people stumbled over narrow ledges where the trail paralleled the river and climbed dangerous cliff trails.

The defiles through which they wound were too narrow for the Kuomintang airplanes to attach them, and the enemy knew their position. So there was no need for concealment. At night they lighted torches made from resin-rich pine boughs cut in the hills. One veteran said later that he could pause at the top of a steep climb and look back over the struggling line of marchers. The flickering torchlight snaked down, around and up the hills in the rear as far as he could see.

"It reminded me of a fiery dragon writhing through the night," he said. Then he added reflectively, "And I suppose in its own way that line of marching men was a dragon of fire."

The Red Army timetable called for reaching Lutingchiao in two days. They begin with straight eight-hour marches followed by four-hour rest periods. In one case, the Kuomintang army was close behind, and Chu Teh pushed his troops through an eighteen-hour march to avoid a fight in open ground. Then, when they got past a narrow defile where the enemy could not flank him, Chu Teh turned and attacked. Spirit overcame the exhaustion of this troops. They won the battle, capturing considerable rice and munitions that they badly needed.

For a time they could see Lin Piao's men marching parallel with them across the river. Then Lin was attacked by a Szechuan force at the same time that Chu Teh's road curved back from the river. They could not tell the outcome of the battle on the opposite bank.

The battles slowed them down, and it was not until the night of the third day that they approached Lutingchiao. Earlier in the evening they glimpsed troops on the other bank at a point where their road curved back along the river. They thought it was Lin Piao's men, whom they had not seen for a day and a half, but then they discovered that it was Szechuan provincial troops. They were under forced march and clearly trying to beat Chu Teh to the Lutingchiao bridge.

Chu Teh called for double time and shorter rests. The weary, lame and wounded found some hidden reserve of strength and gradually pulled ahead of the enemy on the north bank. Chu Teh estimated that they could probably get to the bridge an hour ahead of the enemy.

The big question to Chu now was: Where were Lin Piao and his men? Lin had a radio, but they could not contact him. This could mean that Lin's radio was not working, or that the granite mountains between them were cutting off reception— or that Lin had been destroyed by the enemy.

The Szechuan troops coming up on the north bank did not appear to be large. However, it was impossible to determine exactly how numerous they were. The opposing troops would not have to be very numerous to hold the Lutingchiao bridgehead if they arrived first.

On the other hand, if Lin Piao was still controlling his army and was approaching behind the Szechuan troops, then a Red victory seemed assured. Chu Teh was certain that his side would reach the bridge first, but could they put enough troops across to hold the other end of the bridge before Chiang Kai-shek got in sufficient reinforcements to drive them back?

The town of Lutingchiao was on the north bank of the Tatu River, butting up against the bridgehead. On the south bank, where the Red Army was approaching, there were only a few buildings lining a single road leading to the ancient bridge. An oriental gate-arch framed each end of the bridge. From there, thirteen concrete-anchored chains stretched three hundred yards across the Tatu River chasm. The gorge was narrowed at this point, and that was why Emperor Kang Hsi had selected the location for a bridge in 1701 A.D. The chains were of hammered iron, with links as big in diameter as a rice bowl. All of the chains except four were stretched in parallel lines across the river. Planks were fastened to these chains. The other two chains served as guard rails on each side of the plank flooring.

Chu Teh met no opposition at the south bridgehead, but Nationalist troops in Lutingchiao on the north side had removed the planks from the last two-thirds of the bridge on the south bank. They also had machine gun nests set up to command the chains. The machine gunners were backed by an unknown number of riflemen scattered along the banks in front of the town.

Chu Teh had to make a quick decision. There could be no retreat. Backtracking would throw his forces directly into fresh troops pursuing them. The way ahead along the river was blocked by impassable cliffs.

Chu Teh and Mao held a hasty conference. Then Chu Teh said, "I want some volunteers."

No one had to ask what for. Nothing remained to do but try to swing hand over hand along the chains. That, in the face of the machine guns commanding them, appeared to be pure suicide. Yet an entire company volunteered to try. Chu picked a platoon commander named Ma Ta-Chiu and allowed him to choose the men to go with him. Ma chose not to take his own platoon. His men were too large. Instead he picked at random twenty small, wiry men from Liu Chinkwei's division. Such men would have less weight pulling at their arms as they swung hand over hand along the chain than would heavier men.

Other Red Army troops lined the banks. The roar of the river fighting its way through the narrow gorge was so loud that orders had to be shouted. Other troops were put to work felling trees to use for planks if Ma succeeded in getting across the chains.

Ma prepared his men for their suicide charge. He took their rifles, and they were armed with pistols, hand grenades and long, swordlike knives. They did not carry tommy-guns as one writer claimed. They had to swing monkeylike across the chains. Rifles and machine guns would have hampered their swinging.

When Platoon Leader Ma announced that he was ready to go, word was passed to the Red Army soldiers along the bank. Machine guns and rifles began a steady fire. If they saw a target, they aimed for it. If there were no targets, they fired anyway. Their orders were to create a diversion and to attract as much enemy attention from the chains to themselves as they could.

The twenty men selected to make the crossing moved behind their leader. Ma Ta-chiu paused at the bridgehead to rub his hands in the dirt. This removed body grease and would give him a better grip on the rusty chains.

Ma slipped around the edge of the stone arch and down along the rock and concrete buttress to which the chains were cemented. He bent forward until he could get a good grip on one of the center chains. Then he let himself down until he hung by his hands. His body dangled free above the turbulent river four hundred feet below, which is a distance roughly equal to the height of a forty-story building. He started to swing forward. Behind him, the others grabbed handholds on the chains and followed him. There were not enough chains for each man to use separately. Some doubled up, which caused difficulties. The front man's swing forward jerked the chain. This caused it to sway and throw the back man off-balance.

In principle, swinging across the Tatu chains was no more difficult than a boy's swinging on a school jungle gym. But those were not rigid bars. They swayed and sagged. Wind whistled down the gorge and buffeted the swinging bodies. The chains were rusty and cruelly tore their hands. Death lay four hundred feet below, for nothing could swim in such rough water. Death also waited in front of them. The Szechuan defenders quickly spotted Ma and his men.

The higher elevation of the enemy machine guns was such that the close lines of the twelve chains partially protected the swinging men. The first spray of enemy bullets glanced off the big chain links.

The Red Army machine gunners laid down a furious barrage, trying to protect their men. Red riflemen left cover to get closer to the bank where they could get a better shot.

The Szechuan commander now realized that he made a mistake in leaving part of the bridge planking in place. He had thought that ripping up two-thirds on the opposite side would be enough to stop the Reds. Then there would be less to replace after the battle. The boards were lashed into place by ropes. He knew his men could not survive the murderous Red machine gun fire long enough to untie and remove the rest of the boards. Instead, he ordered them burned. Soldiers ran down and threw kerosene on the planks. Red machine gun fire ripped into them, but not before one got the oil burning.

The Szechuan hero tried to run back to his side, but Red machine gun fire cut him down. The force of the slugs kicked his body off the bridge and into the wild river four hundred feet below. The fire he set blazed up, threatening to burn the remaining planks and to create a blazing barrier to stop Ma and his Red heroes.

Ma's men were still swinging monkeylike along the iron links. One slipped and fell. He made no outcry, but went silently to his death. Another gave a strangled cry as a machine gun slug richochetted off a chain and ripped into the side of his body. A second later, he also was hurtling down into the wild river. Three other men were shot right after him.

A Szechuan soldier managed to climb down beside the buttresses on his side of the bridge. This gave him a straight shot into the swinging line of Red soldiers. He began picking them off one at a time. Ma Ta-chiu, miraculously escaping the rifle fire, tried to swing up off the chains to grab the edge of the burning planks, but Szechuan machine gun fire cut across his chest just as he lifted himself up.

A man, identified in Communist records only as the platoon's political adviser, managed to get off the chains. He was temporarily hidden from the rifleman's view by the boards and from the machine gunners by the almost solid sheet of flame in front of him. He grabbed two hand grenades from his belt. He jerked the pins with his teeth, but held down the arming levers to prevent them from going off. He then crossed his arms over his face to protect his eyes from the flames and charged into the blaze.

His hair singed. His hands scorched, but his clothing did not catch fire. It was too wet with sweat and spray. A startled enemy machine gunner saw him burst through the fire. For a moment the gunner was too surprised to act. That decided the fate of the battle, although fighting would continue for another hour. The gunner's slight hesitation in swinging his gun around gave the political adviser time to hurl his grenades before he was cut in two by enemy fire.

The grenade struck the edge of the forward machine gun nest, and the explosion ripped men and guns to pieces. A Red soldier, trying to follow the political adviser, was knocked off the burning planks by a piece of gun barrel scattered by the explosion.

The Szechuan commander screamed shrilly as he tried to rally his confused troops. Then two other of Ma's men emerged from the blazing bridge. Their grenades ripped another machine gun nest and broke bloody holes in the infantry ranks.

Now other Red soldiers began swinging across the chains. Still more rushed up with logs to lay across it in place of the lost planks. Red engineers worked frantically to get them in place and lashed down.

Agnes Smedley quotes a Red Army staff officer who was with the commander-in-chief: "Chu Teh made no sound, no sign, but stood like a man turned to stone. He knew that the fate of the Red Army was being decided at that moment."

Chu Teh with Mao had climbed to an elevation where they could view the battle. When the Red grenades scattered the enemy machine gun nests, a wild shout went up from the Red infantrymen along the south bank of the Tatu River. Chu Teh and Mao did not join in. From their elevation they could see the approach of the Szechuan troops who had raced them along the river. This put a new element of doubt into the outcome of the crucial battle.

The Red Army was rushing across the Tatu bridge in increasing numbers. They realized as much as Chu Teh that everything depended on this battle. Exhausted though they were, and handicapped by sickness and wounds, they fought with the ferocity of the doomed. But that was not enough. The tide of the battle turned against them. They began to fall back.

The retreat lasted only a few minutes, then suddenly turned to total victory with the arrival at last of Lin Piao's advance troops. Caught now in a squeeze between the two Red armies, the defenders' courage failed. Whole regiments broke and ran. Others threw down their guns and begged for mercy.

There was no rest after that victory. Captured booty from the surrendering Whites had to be sorted and arranged for carrying. Ammunition, guns, food and medical supplies were all Chu Teh bothered with. Other equipment could be used, but he did not want to burden his troops at that crucial point.

After all had crossed the river and had moved into a valley well back of the Tatu, he called a halt for a memorial meeting for the seventeen men who had died forcing the crossing of the Tatu Gorge bridge.

In a speech delivered unsmiling for once, the commander extolled those who had died. Then he told the living and the hardly living that despite the hardships they had endured, the worst was still to come.

"Our difficulties are great," he concluded. "Our enemies are many, but there is no mountain and no river we cannot cross, no fort we cannot conquer."

He then ordered the buglers to sound the advance. The weary horde, less than half of those who left Kiangsi, began to move. In the distance they could see snow-covered peaks blocking their way. Many of those in the ranks had never seen snow. They came from the southern part of China where the climate is subtropical. They had no idea of the terror the icy highland would hold for them.

The day was May 30, 1935, the tenth anniversary of the Shanghai Massacre, when British troops had fired on striking Communists.

8

꒰꒱

The Ice World

Troop morale boomed despite Chu Teh's warning that the worst of the Long March was ahead of them. One of the things contributing to the high spirits was the knowledge that they were only one hundred miles from a junction with Chang Kuo-tao and his Fourth Front Army at Moukung, Szechuan. Most felt that a combination of the two armies would give them the added muscle to soundly defeat Chiang Kai-shek's combined forces.

A hundred miles was about a week's march under normal conditions, or a two-and-a-half day march under forced draft. As it happened, the meeting of the two Communist armies did not take place for another two months.

The first delay was caused by an unexpected battle with Tibetan cavalry from Tachienliu, who had been hired to help the Szechuan provincials. The Red Army lost five hundred men in the fight but gained considerable booty. This included

Tibetan ponies, considerable rice, and silver bullion with which the Chinese had paid the Tibetans for joining in the fight.

After this battle, the First Front Army moved to the foothills of the Payenkala Mountains. There they halted, to prepare for the ordeal ahead. Chu Teh and Mao conferred with natives familiar with the region. They learned that they would encounter only mud and rain on Kuchow, the first mountain. Then they would come to Chiachinshan, the devilish Old Snow Mountain. Here they would have to climb into a land of eternal snow, where they would be menaced by slides, chasms, and narrow, slippery trails.

Mao asked if the trails were passable. The peasants reported that none of them dared attempt it, but that on occasion Tibetan bandits had crossed the glaciers to raid Chinese villages on this side. That was sufficient for Chu Teh. "If they can cross, then the Red Army can cross," he said.

The battle with the Tibetans had been a blessing to the Red Army. It had permitted them to replenish their most-needed supplies. Unfortunately, rice was not in the booty, nor were they able to buy any from the peasants. Rice did not grow well in that cold area. They stocked up on corn, barley, and wheat, plus a plentiful supply of red peppers. The change in diet was hard on stomachs used to rice, and the number of men who contracted intestinal disorders from the new diet was frightening.

The peasants advised them to get furs for the glacial heights. They had a few taken from the Tibetans but were able to buy only a few more. This was not nearly enough warm clothing.

At the start of the Long March each soldier had had one summer and one quilted winter uniform. Most of the winter uniforms had been worn out or lost in battle. Chu Teh issued a lot of captured Nationalist uniforms and told his men to wear them under their Red Army clothings for extra warmth. Each soldier also had a blanket or quilt to sleep on at night. He was told to wrap himself in that if he got cold in the mountains.

Finally the sausage bags were stuffed with wheat, barley or corn, enough to last ten days. Then extra belts of ammunition were issued, although they did not expect any fighting in these mountains. Chu Teh, just before the march resumed, made a final inspection to assure himself that the troops were as warmly clad as possible and had shoes.

The final inspection made, Mao Tse-tung called in his political corps from the surrounding villages, where they had been holding mass Communist indoctrination meetings for the peasants. The "easy" part of the Long March was now over. From this point on, Chu Teh had promised them a worse time than they ever had before—and Chu Teh was an excellent prophet.

They headed for Kuchow Mountain. An attempt to skirt it would involve trying to ford swift mountain rivers gushing down deep defiles. Kuchow was thick with timber. There were no roads—just mountain trails, where the marchers were forced to climb single file along switchback paths that twisted through the trees.

That is a region where the humid air of the subtropical Szechuan and Yunnan basins meets the frigid wind sweeping down from the glacial heights of Chiachinshan. The result is eternal mist, fog and rain. Water dripped constantly from the sea of leaves above them. They were always soaking wet and wading in mud, and they slept in their dripping blankets simply because they were too exhausted to be kept awake by their misery.

Beyond Kuchow they found a valley and stayed there for four days to permit the weaker ones to catch up. The scheduled stop was then extended for a week as they waited for a break in the clouds. It would have been total suicide to head for the frozen heights of Chiachinshan soaking wet.

Finally they got a little sun to dry their clothes and blankets. Then their sausage-bag packs were refilled with another ten days' rations. Chu Teh passed along word for all those able to pack anything else to take along what firewood they could carry. After the rations were distributed, there were some porters and pack animals left whose backs could carry an extra load of firewood.

Chu Teh dispatched an advance team to determine the best passage. The men fanned out over a wide area. Three vanished and were presumed killed. The leader reported back that the best route was a direct climb toward a pass between two peaks straight ahead.

Chu Teh gave the command to march. The columns fell in and began to move slowly. They were all in bad shape. Many could scarcely stagger along. Some kept falling out of ranks to drop on their knees and retch. Some of those in the vanguard ended up with the rear guard. Unable to keep up, they kept stopping to rest and joining whatever next column came along. Progress was very slow.

The weather worsened. They were engulfed in dense fog, followed by rain and hail. The cold increased as they climbed higher. This magnified their suffering beyond anything they had experienced before. Men accustomed to life in the lowlands had difficulty breathing as their columns staggered past the 10,000-foot level. Near the summit they were again hit by hail. The hailstones were as large as baseballs at times. A number of soldiers and pack animals were beaten to death by them.

They could move only a few steps at a time. Then they halted and gasped for breath. The mud was so slippery that they kept falling. Some were so far gone that they never got up.

The columns slowly inched over the summit and down into the valley below. The mountain ahead was still higher and a greater challenge because it was ice-locked. Chu Teh decided on a week's rest, for it was obvious that they would never get over the summit in their present pitiful condition.

Unfortunately, they got only two days' rest. Chiang's reconnaissance planes found them on the second day. Chu Teh knew that that would bring bombers the next day. He passed the order to resume marching. The army wearily picked up its burdens and began moving.

Tales told by survivors of that portion of the march are filled with accounts of terror and unimaginable suffering. There are a number of such accounts, but even so it is difficult to trace their exact route. Events had a tendency to melt together in their numbed minds. They could not recall specific places.

They did agree that the worst barrier was a mountain that reared 16,000 feet in the air. It was completely ice-locked in the upper reaches. Pack animals had difficulty keeping their footing. Hundreds of them slipped into crevasses. The death toll of men ran into the thousands. Some slipped on the ice; some died of complete exhaustion; others froze to death. Fu Lien-chang, a doctor on the Long March, told Nym Wales: "I think our worst problem was the mountain sickness in the Great Snow Mountains. It was caused by rarefied air and the cold."

Another told Agnes Smedley: "The air was so thin we could hardly breathe at all. Speech was impossible. The cold was so dreadful that our breath froze and our hands and lips turned blue. Those who sat down to rest or to relieve themselves froze to death on the spot. Men and animals staggered and fell into chasms and disappeared forever."

At times the air was so still that the travelers could hear feet crunching in the snow for miles. At other times the wind was so furious that the strongest men could not stand before its blast.

Much of the appalling loss of life was due to ignorance. The troops did not know how to survive under arctic conditions. They did not know how to check each other for frostbite or how to use the heat of their hands to thaw frozen patches on their faces and noses.

Neither did they know that one of the great dangers of marching in extreme cold is to avoid getting too hot. When the wind stops and it gets still, it is easy for a climber to raise a sweat under the hard work of plowing through deep snow. Then, when the wind returns or the exhausted climber is forced to rest, the sweat on his body turns to ice and he freezes to death.

They found some relief in the valleys between the icy mountains. It was warmer there, but since it was June, the valley streams were flooded and there was mud everywhere. Once, the rain was so bad that they could not move on for a week.

Eventually they climbed the last of the snow mountains, leaving behind so many dead that no one knew their number any more. Then they came to a valley where they found empty huts of mud and straw and tents made of felted yak wool. The owners had fled at the approach of the Red Army.

The army occupied the empty homes—which was a mixed blessing, for lice were heavy. Despite their exhaustion, army discipline remained strict. Money had to be left in each house to pay for its rental and for the green wheat and barley taken from the fields. Mao tried to communicate with tribesmen in the hills but was not successful. When these efforts failed, Mao had an artist with the army draw pictures showing the benevolence of the Red Army and how it was fighting the Nationalists. The pictures were left, along with the money, in the tribesmen's huts when the Red Army moved on.

They rested three days in that valley and then struggled over the next mountain barrier. The marchers were now in such bad condition that Chu Teh realized they could not go farther without rest. He reluctantly called for a week's halt. He himself caught a cold in the icy mountains, but other than this he came through the ordeal better than any of the others. Even his wife, Kang, was barely able to move.

The troops slept like dead men the first day of the rest. But on the second, Chu Teh had them washing clothes and delousing themselves again. He was far ahead of his time in China in the matter of sanitation.

The evening political sessions and songfests were resumed. They had been neglected during the awful days and nights on the ice mountains. While this went on, Chu and Mao tried to assess the toll that the mountains had taken. The best estimate they could get was between seven and ten thousand.

Their radios were out of commission because of the lack of parts, tubes and batteries, but Chu Teh believed that they were only forty miles from Chang Kuo-tao's Szechuan soviet. At one time this had been second in size only to Mao's Kiangsi soviet. It originated in Honan (not to be confused with Hunan), Hupeh and Anhui provinces, but in 1933 the people there had been driven into Northern Szechuan. Here Chang had been badly mauled in Chiang Kai-shek's Fourth Red Bandit Extermation Campaign. He lost still more territory in the first part of the fifth Nationalist drive.

Now, in July, 1935, Chang Kuo-tao commanded only a quarter of his original soviet, and his hold on that was precarious. However, he did have 50,000 troops who had been well trained by the very able General Hsu Hsiang-chien. These troops made up the Red Fourth Front Army.

Mao and Chu talked over the situation while the First Front Army rested. It now appeared that their only hope was to con-solidate the two armies. If they could weld their exhausted 30,000 troops and Chang's fresh 50,000, they would be in a good position to fight their way through the Nationalist troops they were sure to face in Kansu province before they entered Senshi.

Mao had long resisted the idea of trying to work with Chang Kuo-tao, but he was now willing to bend; the situation was that desperate. Chang held Chu Teh in high regard, both as a man and as a military commander, so there would be no friction between them.

It was imperative that the two armies be joined as soon as possible. Mao did not doubt his army's spirit or its will to fight, but they were all too sick and worn out. They lacked the strength to stand up against fresh troops that Chiang was sure to throw against them.

So Chu Teh had Peng Teh-huai, his second-in-command, take eleven regiments of the men in best condition and push on to reach Chang. The rest of the First Front Army would follow after four more days of rest.

Peng started immediately. He had picked his men with care, but even so they were all in bad physical shape. This slowed his progress more than had been expected. Then, on the fourth day after they left the central army, his columns were moving down a canyon when suddenly there was a rumbling as rocks began rolling down the cliffs upon them. Turning to run, the men were caught by more huge boulders. The rocks crashed through their ranks, crushing those who could not move fast enough to get out of the way.

The rock slides were followed by scattered rifle fire, showing that the slides had not been accidental. Aborigine tribesmen were on the cliffs above the canyon.

Peng pulled back the remnants of his shattered forces, regrouped, and scaled the canyon walls below the aborigines' position. The natives had few guns and could not stand against the Red soldiers' concentrated rush. They fell back and Peng went on.

Shortly after that, however, he found that the retreating aborigines had destroyed a rope bridge across the Black Water River. Peng sent his men scouring the riverbank for five miles downstream to pick up pieces of the cut ropes that had washed down. These were spliced together until enough rope was salvaged to stretch across the stream. One of the few soldiers who could swim carried one end of it to the other bank. After it had been made fast to a tree trunk on each bank, the others used it as a lifeline to cross the river.

On the other side, the men crossed the valley and found their way interrupted by another destroyed bridge. While Peng Teh-huai was deciding what to do, soldiers from Chang's Fourth Front Army appeared on the opposite bank. They helped Peng's men to cross, and there was a joyous reunion between the two Communist groups on the river banks.

This welcome by Chang's fighting men was sincere, but their good feelings did not extend into the higher echelons of the Fourth Front Army. Chang Kuo-tao's hatred of Mao and Chang's personal ambitions would soon pose a new crisis for the weary marchers from Kiangsi.

That problem, however, was still in the future when Peng Teh-huai's troops made their happy contact with Chang Kuo-tao's forward patrols. It appeared to the men from Kiangsi that they had finally come to the end of their Long March.

Peng immediately dispatched runners to carry word to Chu Teh and Mao that contact had been made with the Fourth Front Army. He included a map of the route he had taken, along with a warning about the aborigines. He also got Hsu Hsiang-chien, Chang's military commander, to send engineers out to build bamboo bridges across the two streams the First Front Army would have to cross.

A week later, the central army staggered in. "We wept for joy," a veteran said later. "We thought our troubles were over. We embraced the Fourth Army soldiers, and they cried with us."

The newcomers encamped at Erhokuo, in the Moukung area. The First Front Army soldiers were a direct contrast to their counterparts in the Fourth Front Army on the opposite side of town. They were gaunt. Their faces were lined with starvation, fatigue and suffering. They were ragged and dirty. They shuffled rather than walked. Chang Kuo-tao's Fourth Front soldiers were well fed and well clothed and had obviously done little fighting in recent weeks.

Mao and Chu Teh set up headquarters in one of the village huts. Hsu Hsiang-chien came to see them, but Chang Kuo-tao did not.

The question of command was now a delicate one. Hsu was responsible to Chang, who was political commissar of the Fourth Front Army. At the same time Hsu was also responsible to Chu Teh, who was commander-in-chief of all the Red armies, having been appointed by the Central Committee of the Chinese Communist Party. Mao Tse-tung was chairman of the Central Committee. In that position he was superior to Chang Kuo-tao. However, Mao had to consider Chang's touchy nature—and the fact that Chang's fresh troops greatly outnumbered the exhausted First Front Army.

So Mao made no point of protocol and did not comment on Chang's discourtesy in not coming to welcome them. He also had little to say at the meeting with Hsu Hsiang-chien. Chu Teh carried the conversation. He was most interested in the condition of the Fourth Front Army as a fighting unit. Hsu replied that the soldiers had been recruited in Honan, Anhei and Szechuan. They were all strong peasants and were in excellent condition.

"What about their political conditioning?" Chu Teh asked.

Hsu looked embarrassed. He knew the emphasis both Mao and Chu Teh placed on that. He confessed that the men had not been properly schooled in Communism and its objectives. He also admitted under Chu Teh's sharp questioning that the troops had committed "excesses," as had been reported. By "excesses" he meant that the army had been guilty of looting.

This was in direct conflict with Chu Mao's policy to do nothing that would alienate the peasants.

Mao, however, made no comment. He was still ill with fever. His face was drawn; his eyes were sunk deep in his face. Still, though his clothing was threadbare, it was clean.

Hsu asked about the state of the First Front Army. Actually, Chu Teh did not really know how many men he had left. He thought they numbered about 30,000. Since the Central Army had started from Kiangsi with about 100,000 men and 26 women, that should have placed their losses at around 70,000. However, the army had continually recruited new men along the way, and they were included in the count of the 30,000 survivors.

The entire 30,000-plus had not all been killed. Many of those unable to march on with sickness or wounds had been left with peasants who had promised to help them. There is no way of knowing how many of them survived.

The thing that disturbed Chu Teh most was to learn that Chung Kuo-tao was insisting on special privileges for himself and his officers. In the Central Army, all shared equally. (Riding horses were an exception. Commanders needed them in order to cover more ground in their inspections than they could do on foot.)

After Hsu left, Chu Teh remarked to Mao that it appeared that Chung Kuo-tao was behaving more like a warlord with a private army than as a revolutionary leader of the Chinese Communist Party. Mao did not reply. He looked glum.

Shortly after that Mao took a decisive step. He called a meeting of the Central Committee. He opened the meeting by announcing that they must map plans for a joint march of the two armies into Shensi province.

Chang violently objected. He insisted that the present area, which he dominated, was perfect for a new soviet. It was plain from his manner that he feared he would be dominated by Mao Tse-tung if he went to the northern location.

Mao argued that the Szechuan location was too exposed to Chiang's attacks. Any soviet in that area would be destroyed, as Kiangsi had been, any time Chiang was able to concentrate his full power against it. The bitter argument continued for several days. Chang Kuo-tao finally gave in. He had the Central Committee solidly against him, and he hesitated to defy them all.

Preparation began to resume the march, but it did not start until August, after nearly a month's rest for the First Front Army. The troops started in two separate columns, each of the two armies keeping to itself. Shortly after the start, however, Chang slyly maneuvered so that he ended up with a flooded river between himself and the Chu Mao army.

He then announced that the river was impossible to ford. He intended to return to his position in Szechuan. At the same time he arrested Chu Teh, who had been visiting his command. Chu Teh had brought two corps of men to reinforce Chang for an expected battle with an approaching Kuomintang Army.

There are various stories of what happened next, and they contradict each other. Edgar Snow dismissed it with "There were various other factors of intraparty struggle involved which need not be discussed." Agnes Smedley claims Chang told Chu Teh he could join the Fourth Front Army in turning back or be killed. By Miss Smedley's own admission, this story was hearsay. She did not get it from Chu Teh, although she knew him well.

Chang was a far-from-stupid man, and it seems incredible that he would have considered executing Chu Teh. Chu Teh was so popular that any violence against him would have turned Chang into an outlaw with all the Communist Party.

Another story claims that Chu Teh's two First Front corps were ready to fight for his release and Chu Teh agreed to go with Chang to avoid civil war between the two armies. This account had the advantage of keeping the situation from looking as though Chu Teh had agreed to abandon Mao for Chang.

Still another account claims that Mao secretly sent Chu Teh word to agree with Chang in order to avoid conflict. Also, the story goes, Mao felt that Chu Teh would gradually undermine Chang and bring the Fourth Front Army to Shensi without strife.

In any event, Chu Teh and the two Central Army corps went back with Chang Kuo-tao. The First Front Army, with Peng Teh-huai and Lin Piao in the top command slots, resumed their march toward Shensi on the border of faraway Mongolia.

They were moving directly toward the land of the hard-fighting Mantzu tribesmen and the bitter Hsifan of Tibet. And beyond these tribesmen's lands, where so many would die, were the weird Grasslands, which—in a different way— would be as awful an ordeal to traverse as the Great Snow Mountain had been.

9

❧

The Great Grasslands

The month's rest had helped the First Front Army. They resumed the Long March with renewed enthusiasm. They knew they would have to fight the Mantzus but did not consider them a real obstacle. Later they would learn to their sorrow that the Mantzus were the hardest fighters they had ever encountered.

Mao Tse-tung did not share the high spirits of his command. He missed Chu Teh, and, while his fever had abated, he was still weak and tired most of the time. He was particularly worried about the split caused by Chang Kuo-tao's pullout. That division of the Party's armies would make it easier for Chiang Kai-shek's next Extermination Campaign.

Mao also had his own position to consider. His failure to unite the Party at Moukung would be held against him. He knew from bitter experience how easily a Party leader could be replaced. This had happened to Li Li-san, who had led the

Party in its opening campaigns to organize city workers. It had happened to Chou En-lai, who had been the Military Council chairman until he was replaced by Mao at Tsunyi. Much earlier, Mao also had been removed from a high Party position because his views conflicted with those of his fellow committeemen.

He knew that his Party enemies were waiting now for him to make a major mistake. Then he would be replaced, possibly with Chang Kuo-tao—or the Bolsheviks might regain power.

Mao's entire life had been a succession of ups and downs. He expected more. What he feared was the destruction of his policy to abandon city workers and to concentrate on agrarian revolt among the peasants.

Mao knew that there was still much opposition to his policies in the Party. Some of his opponents had voted for him as chairman to replace Po Ku because they hoped he would fail as they had previously failed. This would pave the way for their return and a reinstatement of the Russian-backed worker organization policy.

Mao was convinced that such an outcome would wreck the Communist Party. A workers' policy had succeeded in Russia. The Russian-trained "Returned Students," along with Stalin, could not realize that conditions were different in China. The country was not industrialized. It had not enough of the class of people the Russian-trained segment of the Party wanted to organize. Also, the foreign elements were too deeply entrenched in the cities; they would resist a Communist takeover, as the British had broken the Communist strike in Shanghai in 1925.

The problem, in Mao's eyes, was Karl Marx's contempt for the peasant as a revolutionist. Marx had considered the farmer as nothing but a bread source for the working proletariat; Mao believed that agrarian revolt was the only way Communism could succeed in China. As a result he had concentrated on the peasants since 1927. Later, he would betray them, stripping away their precious land and forcing them into communes when private ownership of lands failed to feed China's 800-million-plus hungry mouths. But at this point Mao was firmly committed to an agrarian revolt. His problem was to keep control in order to move the Party in that direction.

As Mao Tse-tung wrestled with that problem, his soldiers moved confidently into the tribal lands of the Mantzu tribes. Mao had always had extraordinary luck in dealing with the minority groups of China, winning them to the Communist side with his policy of autonomous minority territories. He had no cause to believe he would fail now. He expected fighting in the beginning, which had happened with the Lolos at first. This the army was prepared for. Chu Teh was gone, but Mao himself had had considerable experience in directing an army before he joined with Chu Teh, and he became an outstanding authority on guerrilla warfare. With him were Lin Piao, acknowledged to be a tactical genius, and Peng Teh-huai, who was an exceptional battlefield commander. Lo Ping-hui, who had done such a magnificent job with the rear guard, had been cut off by rising rivers and had turned back to join Chang and Chu Teh.

It was a shock, then, for the Red army to find that they were unable to make any kind of friendly contact with the Mantzus or with the Hsifan-Tibetans who lived just beyond the Mantzu region. Worse yet, the Mantzus acted as if they had sat at the feet of Chu Mao during guerrilla warfare lectures. They employed the very same tactics against the Red Army that the Communists had employed against Chiang Kai-shek's Kuomintang—and were just as successful.

It will be remembered that Communist military tactics were based on the principles:

- When the enemy advances, retreat.
- When the enemy halts, plague him.
- When the enemy tries to avoid battle, attack him.
- When the enemy retreats, pursue him.

When fighting the Kuomintang, the Red Army often broke into numerous guerrilla units to harass the enemy from a hundred separate points. Chiang Kai-shek's troops could not fight except as a mass unit. If they broke into small groups to pursue the hit-and-run Red guerrillas, they would be cut down by vengeful peasants and partisan fighters.

Now this was happening to the Red Army in Mantzuland. All the local natives were united against the invaders. As the Red Army advanced, the Mantzus retreated, taking with them everything transportable. They left crops growing in the fields, but the planting season is late in those high valleys. None of the crops were ripe. The Red Army was able to gather only some green grain and a few half-grown vegetables.

Lin Piao tried pursuing the retreating Mantzus, hoping to seize some of the cattle they were driving away. Invariably his pursuit parties were cut off by swift-moving Mantzus astride hardy little Tibetan ponies. They would ride out of the hills and circle the Red companies to harrass them like Indians attacking a wagon train in the American West. They hit unexpectedly and were gone before the confused Communists could rally to fight back.

Previously the Red Army had marched strung out. Sometimes there had been several days' marches between the advance group and the rear guard. Now they were forced to group and march in tight formation.

Things worsened when they moved into the mountains again as the vengeful tribesmen loosened landslides and rolled huge boulders onto the struggling Red columns. One great rock killed twenty men and seven pack animals.

There were no big, pitched battles, but the constant whittling away cost the Reds more men than they had lost in their biggest battle with Chiang Kai-shek's Whites. There was little they could do about it except keep watch and strike back at the ghostlike enemy they could never seem to get in their gunsights.

As Edgar Snow reported, "Here were no chances to explain 'Red policy toward national minorities,' no opportunities for friendly alliance. The Mantzu queen had an implacable hatred for Chinese of any variety and recognized no distinction between Red and White. She threatened to boil alive any one who helped the travelers."

In ten days they were out of Mantzuland, but that time had proven to be the worst ten days in the history of the Red Army's fighting. Chou En-lai is said to have remarked after that ordeal that he understood now how the Kuomintang felt when the Red Army attacked them, ran, and then circled back to attack again from a different and unexpected angle.

But difficult as those ten days had been, the next ten were absolutely frightful. The marchers had heard of the region called *Tsao ti*, or the Great Grasslands, but none of them was prepared for what it actually turned out to be. Agnes Smedley described it in this way:

"As far as the eye can reach, day after day, the Red Army saw nothing but an endless ocean of high wild grass growing in an icy swamp of black muck and water many feet deep.... No tree or shrub grew here, no bird ventured near, no insect sounded. There was nothing, nothing but endless stretches of wild grass swept by torrential rains ... "

As they neared this forbidding area, the Mantzu tribesmen made one last attack. They stormed out of the hills on their ponies to strike at the Red Army rear guard. The attack was beaten back, but a hundred Red soldiers were killed.

The important thing about that final battle with the Mantzus was that the Reds captured twenty of the enemy, their first Mantzu captives. Mao, who rarely showed emotion, was jubilant. He hoped to win them over as he had the Lolos. Then he hoped to send them back to Mantzuland as Communist missionaries.

However, the captives proved to be of greater value as guides than as future Communist teachers. When they could find no way to enter the Great Grasslands bogs, the Red advance guard drove the captive Mantzus ahead of them into the mud. The tribesmen tried to bluff. They advanced until they sank to their waists in the icy black goo under the sea of grass.

The prisoners threw up their hands to indicate that it was death to go farther; they would sink over their heads. The guards motioned with their rifles, indicating that they should pull up bunches of grass and pile it on the mud as a mat.

Convinced at last that the mad Hans (Chinese) were determined to go ahead regardless of the consequences, the captives gave in. They felt that it was better to show these crazy men a way out, for in that way they would be rid of them more quickly. They motioned to show that they wanted to move to a new location. Then they led their captors to an almost invisible trail that followed a hard ridge through the strange swamp.

The rest of the army followed. It was only September, but already cold winds and rain were sweeping down from the high Tibetan plateaus. The rain was torrential. The foot path they followed did not run straight. It branched, doubled back, and almost disappeared. In places it sank under the tarry muck, and the marchers floundered up to their hips in the icy mud. Animals bogged down and had to be pulled out by straining men who could scarcely pull their own feet out of the mess. Some men became confused and slipped off the trail. They sank in over their heads and were never seen again.

The long line of marchers struggled on for ten hours, slipping, sliding, and struggling against wind, rain and mud. They were unable to find a solid area to camp on. Instead, they had to bed down on the trail. Some flopped in the mud and slept from sheer exhaustion. Others cut some of the four-foot-high grass, tied it in shocks, and built themselves a grass tent that helped to shelter them from wind and rain.

The wind was raw and cold. The miserable men pulled wet blankets around themselves for some protection and huddled together until morning.

At dawn they tried to eat some of the green wheat in their sausage bags. Some of it had molded and had a foul odor. Some retched after eating it. Some coughed blood. Others sat and stared dumbly at hideous sores and unhealed wounds that were being made worse by the filthy mud they waded through.

The same punishment went on day after day. The mud sucked at their legs so that each step was a major effort. The death toll reached a thousand a day, far exceeding an average battle loss. Yet the survivors found strength each day to stumble ahead on trembling legs.

One soldier later told a bitter story about how his companion suddenly sagged in his arms. Unable to hold up the fainting man, he let him sink down prone in the mud. Then, thinking that his friend needed food, he took the last handful of wheat from his pack. The unfortunate man looked at it dumbly. He reached out with a trembling hand to take the few pitiful grains, but shuddered and died.

The man who tried to help him put the wheat back in his pack, leaving the dead man sprawled in the mud. Later, when his squad stopped for another miserable rest, he took out the wheat that he had offered to the dead man. It was all he had left. He thought of the dead man . . . "And I couldn't eat that wheat," he said.

Mao still had his horse, but the narrow trail was too dangerous to ride. He trudged along, slopping through the thick mud along with the others. His head was bowed. His face was glazed with mud and streaked by rain. Every so often he would reach back and touch his knapsack as if to assure himself that his precious maps and plans were still with him.

Chou En-lai often walked with Mao. Lin Piao and Peng Teh-huai were with the advance guard. Lin had had trouble with his weak heart while crossing the snow mountains, and it was troubling him again. The German "Li Te" (Otto Braun) struggled along with Mao. He did not seem to resent being deposed as the master tactician. Often he and Mao experimented with different plants along the way, seeking substitutes for the tobacco they craved. Red Army policy did not forbid tobacco, but its use was discouraged in talks to the young soldiers. This was one place where the rule that all shared alike failed. Chu Teh and Mao were both chain smokers, and it has been reported that Chu Teh often had a cigarette in his mouth as he lectured the young soldiers on the evils of smoking.

On the afternoon of the tenth day they were electrified to hear shots in the distance. The rain had temporarily stopped, although the dark clouds still bellied low with a promise of another downpour soon. The entire army was now nothing but a mob of living skeletons in muddy rags. But the sound of gunfire ahead jolted them back into some semblence of a fighting force again. They had been sloughing through the mud with their rifles slung barrel-down to keep rainwater from getting inside. Now they shifted their weapons to the alert and stumbled forward in as much of a run as their shaking legs could produce.

Shortly, they came at last to the end of the awful Grasslands. Beyond, the ground was firm and they found a village of mud huts from which the Hsifan tribesman had fled. Here they were able to rest a little, bathe, and clean their clothes in the rain. They gathered some vegetables from gardens deserted by the fleeing natives.

They thought they could rest then, for Shensi province, their final goal, was just over the Chungling mountains. But their advance guards reported that Chiang Kai-shek had pushed his 49th Division under Hu Tsung-nam into the corner of Kansu Province, which they had to cross to get to Shensi.

Despite all they had suffered, the Central Army smashed through the Kuomintang's 49th Division, only to encounter a Kansu provincial army commanded by Lu Ta-chang.

Hu's 49th Division had lacked the will to fight and had given up easily, but the Kansu troops were of sterner stock. Like the Mantzus, they fought by occupying the high cliffs, to shoot and roll boulders down on the stunned Reds.

That was almost the final blow. There is a limit to human endurance. But the habit of fighting back despite all odds was so deeply engrained that the exhausted army again found a hidden reserve of strength. While part of them stood fast, shooting back at the solidly entrenched Kansus, some rear units fell back out of sight of the enemy on the cliffs. Their orders were to scale the cliffs and attack the enemy from the back.

The rock walls of the gorge were unscalable, it seemed. There were no trails anywhere, nor could the men find any broken surfaces where they could get toe and handholds.

However, they remembered having seen some trees growing in the sheer cliff about two miles back. Seeds in years past had blown into cracks in the rocks and had grown. Returning to that spot, the men tied strings to rocks and tried to throw them over the branches of the lowest tree. Their idea was to use the strings to pull ropes up and around the tree trunks for scaling ladders. Unfortunately, the trees were growing too high on the cliff; nobody could throw that high.

From down the narrow canyon they could hear the echo of gunfire from their stalled comrades. The regiment's commander gave the order to backtrack still farther in hope of finding someplace to scale the cliff. Then someone had another idea. Following his suggestion, they improvised a bow and arrow from branches of heavy bushes along the bottom of the draw and attached string to the arrow. After several tries they got their missile over a solid branch of one of the high trees and the arrow fell back to earth, leaving their loop of twine over the tree. Rope was hastily pieced together, tied to the string, and pulled up until a cluster of special knots on the rope was jammed into a fork of the tree.

The first man chosen to climb the rope got halfway up and fell when his strength gave out. Two more were also unsuccessful before one man managed to reach the tree on the cliff face. From there he was able to get toeholds in the rocks and work himself laboriously to the top.

The men were so weakened by semistarvation that only fourteen of the fifty were able to make the grueling climb. Those who made it to the top spread out in a skirmish line and attached the rear rank of the Kansu provincials on the cliff. They went into battle with loud screams, rapid firing, and as much noise as possible, to give the effect of a larger force.

When the startled Kansuans fell back in momentary confusion, the main force of the Central Army in the defile surged forward. Several companies had gotten past before the Kansu commander realized that he faced only a handful of men on the cliff. He rallied his troops and they destroyed the gallant fourteen. Then he got his men back into position commanding the pass below.

Hasty gunfire and rolling rocks again ripped into the Red ranks as they rushed past the blockade area. About two hundred died in that encounter, but those who had passed double-timed it down the canyon until they found a way up the cliff and circled back to attack the Kansuans. Now faced with a larger Red force on the cliff, the Kansu regiments turned to meet the new danger, and this permitted the remainder of the Red Army to pass. They routed the enemy, smashing the last barrier between themselves and Shensi.

Now they moved over the border mountains into Shensi and on to the town of Paoan, where they held a joyous reunion with soldiers of the Shensi soviet. Some men shouted. Some laughed. And some were so overcome by emotion that they broke out in deep, wracking sobs. It was said that even Mao Tse-tung's reserve broke. There were tears in his eyes as he stooped and dug his fingers into the loess soil, crumbling it almost lovingly in his hands.

His voice was so thick that those about him could scarcely understand his words as he said, "If we can survive all this, we can survive everything. This is but the first stage of our Long March. The final stage leads to Peking!"

The Red Army was home at last. They had walked for a year and two days since leaving Kiangsi, covering eight thousand miles. Six thousand of this was the direct route. Maneuvering and backtracking accounted for the extra two thousand.

In their year-long retreat they had struggled up and across eighteen mountain ranges, five of them glacially locked in eternal ice and snow. They had crossed twenty-four major rivers and fought some kind of battle or skirmish on an average of once a day.

They had left Kiangsi with about 100,000 men; no authority has agreed on the exact number. They arrived in Shensi with 20,000. This number included those who had been recruited and trained during the March. Enlistments accounted for a considerable number and made up the bulk of those finally arriving in Shensi. The best estimate of the number of original Kiangsi soldiers who finally reached Shensi is 7,000. Probably about 2,000 of the original group were with Chu Teh in northwest Szechuan. No estimate can be made as to the survival of the wounded left with peasants along the way.

But the arrival of the Central Army—the First Front Army—in Shensi did not end the Long March, for Ho Lung and Chang Kuo-tao, as Mao had predicted, had to abandon their soviets and follow the bitter trail broken for them by the heroic men from Kiangsi.

10

~

What Came After

The escape of the Central Army into Shensi was a disappointment to Chiang Kai-shek. However, he did not consider it a threat to him in such a remote area, so he threw the bulk of his armies into an extermination campaign against the remaining soviets in Hunan and Szechuan.

At this time the Japanese, who had invaded Chinese Manchuria in 1932, were encroaching on China proper. Instead of fighting the Japanese invaders, Chiang retreated before their advance and used his armies against the Chinese Communists. He considered them a greater threat to him personally.

The result was that Ho Lung was forced to evacuate his soviet in Hunan about the time the First Front Army of Mao Tse-tung was arriving in its Shensi sanctuary. Ho had the advantage of information about the Mao Long March. As a result, he followed the Central Army's path through

Kweichow and Yunnan, living off the land as Chu Teh and Mao had done. But he decided that swinging into the Tibetan plateau was preferable to trying to cross the five glacial mountains where so many of the First Front Army had frozen to death.

Swinging around this great barrier, Ho Lung finally made contact with Chang Kuo-tao and Chu Teh in what was then Sikang but is now western Szechuan. Chang and Chu Teh were also being cut to pieces by Chiang's advances. For some time Chu Teh had been trying to persuade Chang to move north and join Mao at Paoan in Shensi. Ho Lung now added his argument to that of Chu Teh. Chang, realizing at last that Mao Tse-tung had been right about his inability to sustain a soviet in Szechuan, reluctantly agreed to join the Second Front Army (Ho Lung's group) in completing its Long March to Shensi.

The three armies finally joined together in Shensi in October, 1936. Their combined Long March had taken two full years. According to what Chou En-lai told Edgar Snow, the Red Army strength then totaled 35,000 men. It is likely that Chou, not wanting Chiang Kai-shek to learn the exact number of the Red Army, deliberately understated the number. The total appears to have been closer to 60,000 with constant recruiting gradually swelling the number.

The Long March had solidly entrenched Mao and his supporters. He was not a total dictator, however, but was considered by other members of the Central Committee as "an equal among equals." He continued without opposition to set the basic policies of the Communist Party and retained his post of Party Chairman through all the ups and downs that followed.

The Communists gained strength in Shensi. Fighting continued, but it was sporadic and mostly against provincial troops. Eventually, the Red Army captured Yenan, the Shensi capital, and made that ancient walled city the Party head-quarters.

Now that his forces were free from the threat of constant battle and were rapidly regaining strength, Mao abruptly changed policy. Instead of fighting the Kuomintang army, he tried to bring about a coalition with them to fight the Japanese, who were advancing deeper into China. Mao felt that the only way the Japanese invaders could be beaten was for the Kuomintang and the Red Army to fight together against them. But Chiang refused. He still felt the Communists were his greater enemy.

The situation came to a head when Chiang attempted to use the "Young Marshal" Chang Hsueh-Iiang to mount an attack on Yenan. Chang Hsueh-liang was called the "Young Marshal" to distinguish him from his father, the "Old Marshal," who had been warlord of Manchuria until he was killed by a Japanese bomb in 1928.

After the Young Marshal was run out of Manchuria by the Japanese invasion in 1932, he set up headquarters in Sian, a city south of Yenan, and supported Chiang Kai-shek. However, the Young Marshal became increasingly dissatisfied with Chiang's refusal to fight the Japanese. So when Chiang Kai-shek flew to Sian in December, 1936, to enlist the Young Marshal's aid in driving the Red Army out of Yenan, Chang Ksueh-liang put Chiang Kai-shek under arrest. He threatened to execute Chiang unless the Kuomintang joined the Communist in a United Front against the Japanese.

Chiang refused. Mao Tse-tung was almost frantic. Stalin was also greatly concerned. They all put pressure on the Young Marshal to prevent Chiang Kai-shek's execution. While Mao hated Chiang, he feared the Japanese invasion more, and he knew that neither the Red Army nor the Kuomintang Army could defeat the Japanese alone. The future of China depended on a United Front.

Chiang finally gave in. For the next two years the Nationalists and the Communists cooperated in fighting the common Japanese enemy. But from 1939 on, Chiang increasingly adopted a policy of retreating before the Japanese. Mao charged that Chiang was saving the Kuomintang Army for another Communist extermination campaign when the war with Japan ended. Chiang's reluctance to fight became more pronounced after Pearl Harbor brought the United States into the war.

Millions in supplies were flown into China from U.S. bases in India and carried over the Burma Road to Chungking. Still Chiang refrained from fighting the Japanese whenever he could. He called his defeatist policy "trading space for time," as the Japanese advanced.

After the war, the United States tried to bring Mao and Chiang together in a coalition government. This failed, and fighting resumed between the Communists and Chiang's Nationalists. Then, on February 3, 1949, Mao—standing upright in the front of a captured Jeep—rode into Peiping (Peking). Chu Teh rode in another Jeep directly behind him.

Fighting continued after the fall of the Nationalist capital, but by October 1 Mao was able to proclaim the People's Republic of China. They now controlled the entire mainland. Chiang and his followers fled to Taiwan to form the rival Republic of China.

The Long March was finally over.

When the Long March had began in October, 1934, the Communists had been beaten and their Party had been on the verge of destruction. The final Red victory came about because of three things that happened during the Long March from Kiangsi to Shensi:

1. Mao Tse-tung was able to gain control from the Russian-dominated Central Committee, eliminating poor tactics and policies.

2. By adroit maneuvering and skillful fighting, the Red Army was able to preserve a nucleus of a fighting force upon which to rebuild their strength.

3. And Mao, through his political commissars, made his cause known to 200,000,000 people during the Long March and was able to convince them that the Communists were on their side.

This last was of extreme importance. During the Long March the Communists traversed areas where the people had not known anything about them except through Nationalist propaganda, which pictured the Red Army as another bandit group that exploited the farmers.

Mao's policy of treating the peasants as friends, insisting that the Red Army pay for everything taken from them and distributing to hungry peasants the surpluses taken from rich landlords, as well as his continual mass political meetings, paid off when the big Communist push came after World War II. The Reds got full peasant support. Prior to the Long March, Mao had worked with peasants of Hunan, Kiangsi and Anhwei, but the Long March gave him the invaluable contact with that extra 200 million in Kweichow, Yunnan, Szechuan, and Kansu, in addition to the aborigine tribes.

One can also see in the Long March the roots of the conflict today between Red China and Red Russia. At Tsunyi Mao definitely turned his back on Russian domination of the Chinese Communist Party. It is significant that Stalin continued to support Chiang Kai-shek long after Chiang began fighting the Chinese Communists. In 1947 Stalin told General George Marshall of the U.S. Mission to China that the Chinese Communists were "radishes—red on the outside but white inside."

China needed foreign friends and tried to make peace with Russia. This may have been what was behind the move that forced Mao to resign as president of the Republic in 1959, al-

though he retained his title of Party Chairman. According to
John Roderick, chief of the Far East Bureau of Associated
Press, Mao complained that he was not consulted on any
major matter between 1959 and 1966. The Party was controlled by Liu Shao-chi, a man who kept well in the background as he built his power, and Teng Hsaio-ping, the
Party's Secretary-General. Both men were pro-Russian.

Then, in 1966, with the Party again in trouble, Mao won a
crucial election in the Central Committee just as he had done
at Tsunyi during the Long March. Roderick reported that it
was eighty-year-old Chu Teh who cast the deciding vote in
favor of a new takeover by Mao Tse-tung.

There was considerable opposition to Mao's election victory
by Liu and Teng, but Mao was backed by the ambitious Lin
Piao and the Red Guard bands of Chinese youth. Mao
emerged victor in the fight, which he termed the "Cultural
Revolution." It is significant that the new Party constitution
then specified that Lin Piao would be Mao's successor as Party
Chairman.

Apparently Lin Piao backed Mao only to further his personal ambition, for suddenly in September, 1971, Lin fled
from Peking in a plane bound for Moscow. The plane crashed
in Mongolia, killing Lin and his companions. His death was
followed by nine months' silence. Then an announcement was
made that Lin Piao had tried to assassinate Mao Tse-tung
and seize power himself. At that time Lin was Minister of
Defense.

The defection of Lin Piao put Chou En-lai, another of the
Long Marchers, in the number two spot to succeed Mao. The
Red Army is now under Chen Chien-ying, who also was on
the Long March. Thus comrades of the epic retreat are still
solidly in command in China today. But they are all growing
old. Chu Teh, at 86, is said to be senile. Mao Tse-tung is 79.
Chen Chien-ying is 74, and Chou En-lai is 72.

Although the Old Guard is dying off, the Long March will still be remembered. In Peking there is a revolutionary museum where relics of the Long March are preserved. Included is a giant relief map, which lights up to show the route and each stage where the marchers stopped. A hidden speaker delivers a recorded account of the ordeal and what it means to modern China.

As for Mao himself, his opinion of the epic retreat is summed up in a statement he made soon after it ended:

"Since Pan Ku divided heaven and earth and the Three Sovereigns and the Five Emperors reigned, has there ever been in history a Long March like ours?"

BIBLIOGRAPHY

Edmonds, I. G., *Revolts and Revolutions*. New York, Hawthorn Books, Inc., 1969.

Emi Siao, *Mao Tse-tung, His Childhood*. Bombay, India, n. d.

Goldston, Robert, *The Rise of Red China*. New York, Bobbs-Merrill, 1967.

Isaacs, Harold R., *Tragedy of the Chinese Revolution*. Stanford, Stanford University Press, 1966.

Jen Yu-ti, *Consice Geography of China*. Peking, China, Foreign Language Press, 1964.

Payne, Robert, *Mao Tse-tung*. New York, Abelard Schuman, 1962.

Roderick, John, *What You Should Know About the People's Republic of China*. New York, The Associated Press, 1972.

Robottom, John, *China in Revolution*. New York, McGraw-Hill, Inc., 1967.

Rue, John E., *Mao Tse-tung in Opposition*. Stanford, Stanford University Press, 1966.

Smedley, Agnes, *The Long Road*, New York, Monthly Review Press, 1956.

Snow, Edgar, *Red Star Over China*. New York, Random House, 1938.

Wales, Nym, *Red Dust*. Stanford, Stanford University Press, 1952.

INDEX

INDEX

147